NEPANTLA

NEPANTLA

Essays from the Land

in the Middle

PAT MORA

University of New Mexico Press

Albuquerque

First paperbound printing, 2008

Paperbound ISBN: 978-0-8263-4527-1

Printed in the United States of America

13   12   11   10   09   08   1   2   3   4   5   6

Library of Congress Cataloging in Publication Data

Mora, Pat.

Nepantla: essays from the land in the middle / Pat Mora.–1st ed.

p. cm.

Includes index.

ISBN 0–8263–1454–6

1. Mora, Pat—Biography. 2. Poets, American—20th century—
Biography. 3. Mexican Americans—Civilization. I. Title.

PS3563.073Z472 1993

811.'54—dc20

[B]   92–39874

CIP

The author thanks Arte Público Press for permission to quote from her following poems:
"Foreign Spooks," "Petals," "Desert Women," "Bailando," "Fences," "Don Jaime,"
"Abuelita Magic," "Diagnosis," "Immigrants," "Elena," "My Word-house,"
"*Mañanitas*: Birthday Song," "Too Many Eyes," "Dominican Gold,"
"Bribe," "*Bruja*: Witch," "Curandera," "1910," and "Tree-wisdom."
She also wishes to acknowledge the publication of previous versions of the following
essays: "Living on the Border," *The Christian Science Monitor*; "To Gabriela, a Young
Writer," *English Journal* and *The Horn Book Magazine*; "Endangered Species," *Vista* and
Impresión; "Island Images," *Focus*; "Unseen Teachers," *CALYX*; and "Snapshots," "Lobo,"
and "Desert Women," *Impresión*.

The Introduction contains poetry passages from *Adobe Odes* by Pat Mora.

Book design by Kristina E. Kachele

CONTENTS

INTRODUCTION

Dear Readers,

How grateful I feel for the healthy, busy years since I first welcomed you to this word-house. I lived in Cincinnati when I worked on *Nepantla*. Those years in southern Ohio and later across the Ohio River in northern Kentucky were the only time I lived away from the Southwest. I enjoyed cardinals, maples, and oaks, but did I miss mountains and hearing Spanish. I was born and spent much of my life in El Paso, situated in low-desert terrain; now I live in beautiful Santa Fe, in the cooler and, grumble, grumble, winter-freezing, high desert. *¡Qué frío!*

Above my computer, I see foothills the color of ground cinnamon, dotted with piñon and juniper trees. No longer am I in the "middle" in the ways mentioned when this book was first published. I'm not in the middle of my life, of the country, nor between my mother and daughters. Though Mom and Dad are no longer physically on this earth, I assure you that *mis padres*, like my beloved aunt, Lobo, are with me daily. Like many bilinguals, I will always be in the middle between those who speak only English or only Spanish.

I was surprised to notice that when *Nepantla* was published, only one of my children's books had been. Writing for children and speaking to educators is now a significant, joyful part of my life, as is the family literacy initiative we call "Día," El día de los niños / El día de los libros, Children's Day / Book Day. Becoming a literacy advocate evolved from my personal love of reading (inspired by Mom) and from my desire to inspire my fellow readers to share "bookjoy."

Many creative and energetic librarians, teachers, authors, and illustrators have a daily commitment to "Día," creating a national Día community that celebrates children and revels in linking them to books, languages, and cultures, culminating in a national celebration on April 30th. Language and languages offer pleasure but also power. The term "democracy" will become hollow if we're not a literate society of critical thinkers—so needed in our world still violent and unjust.

Since I like people of all ages and enjoy listening to them and their stories, I enjoy sliding back and forth between publishing books for children, teens, and for adults—thirty children's books, a teen poetry collection, and for adults: a family memoir and three more poetry collections since *Nepantla* was first published. I've also completed a book of letters to educators on creativity. The challenges of writing for various age groups are different, but the pleasures equal. (Children doubt this since they can't imagine why I wouldn't far prefer to write for them.)

I keep a journal when I travel out of the country, so I have notes and even drafts of essays about my trips these last years, but I haven't even had time to reread what I wrote. I wish I'd had the opportunity to polish and publish essays about those travels since writing helps me see what I saw and think about what I experienced, such as editing and adding to *Agua Santa: Holy Water* looking out at the Aegean. Editing *Adobe Odes* on the edge of Lake Towada, a volcanic lake in Japan, I wrote of our human connectedness,

A crow caws here
and in Santa Fe the same sun sets
behind a mountain. . . .

I feel fortunate to have spent even brief time these last years in France, Belize, Germany, Brazil, and Finland. I smile at singing "Old McDonald Had a Farm" in 1993 to Chinese children in a rural village. That song was the one everyone in our U.S. group knew. We certainly made those sweet children laugh.

I remember struggling to make flower offerings in Bali, my teacher a patient woman who let me sit on the platform outside her small home and clapped enthusiastically when I did anything remotely right. And how my husband Vern and I enjoyed our good fortune, writing for weeks in a real castle in Umbria, our shower in a turret.

Although I feel thirty-five, I'm technically sixty-five, which I frankly find astonishing. Both Mom and Lobo prepared me for this sensation since they'd say about their ages, "But, dear, I don't feel that old." I tease my three wonderful grown children that it's biologically amazing that they are older than I am. I long for balance in all our lives now, exercising not only our minds, but our bodies and spirits. I seek quiet, time to pray, meditate, develop compassion, gratitude, joy; time to ponder what my work is in this world.

I hope that you enjoy these ruminations, dear readers, and that they inspire you to raise *your* voice and to embrace both action and *la esperanza*, hope, for

> Each day, we rise, reborn,
> our round rhythm:
> another chance.

For my fine editor, Andrea Otañez,
who believed in this book,
a woman who listens, thinks, cares.

NEPANTLA

I

BIENVENIDOS

Welcome to "My Word-house."

The walls grow out of the desert
naturally, like *agave, nopal,* yucca.
Vines, winds and strangers enter large, bare
rooms with ease, no private entrances, no secret locks,
just rough *álamo* slabs framing windows and doors.
. . . .
In the kitchen, family bread is always rising.[1]

Why is a woman who loves the Chihuahua desert writing in
Cincinnati, Ohio? I'm doing what all writers do: writing where
I find myself. I began this manuscript when summer heat was
beginning to wane, when I was about to witness my second Midwest fall. I took long walks and returned dizzy from the whirl
of gold. Fall is a reflective season, a good time for mulling. It
proved a good time to begin rethinking these essays, some of
which began as speeches given during my years in university
administration.

Prior to 1989 I had always lived in my native El Paso, Texas.
I was a student at the local university, at which I eventually

3

became an administrator after years spent teaching, then parenting, and eventually teaching again. The seemingly endless stacks of essays to read and a growing desire to write finally convinced me to apply for a position that might require a long day, but allow evenings and weekends for my children and my writing. The years as a high school teacher, and as a community college and university instructor, left me with supreme respect for those who devote themselves to teaching with enthusiasm year after year.

Why are you marking someone else's papers? I would ask myself during the last semesters of teaching freshman English. I thought, You need to be marking your own work. Although it is often fashionable for faculty to speak of administrative work and administrators disparagingly, I enjoyed certain aspects' of those years between 1981 and 1989 when I was assistant to the vice-president for academic affairs, director of the university museum, and assistant to the president. Cultural conservation, communication, leadership, and change—both personal and societal—all interest me. Universities can and should play pivotal roles in enriching the life of a community, and I was fortunate to work on issues of outreach to women and to the local Mexican American population. The campus that virtually ignored my cultural heritage when I was a student had to change to survive during the late eighties as the Chicano population of El Paso grew steadily. What an identity crisis the university had, much as individuals often do, when we finally confront our true selves. Often reluctantly, the university had to say its true name—that of an institution serving a border population. The denigration of Mexico and Mexican heritage along the longest border in the world made that admission painful. For those of us committed to extending the opportunities of the university to our community, it was a frustrating but exciting time to participate in that gradual transformation.

In completing this book, I hoped to gather some of my work in a manner that might be useful to Latinas and to those concerned with us. I admit somewhat wistfully that not all readers find the pleasure and solace in poetry that I do. The essay format allows me to explore a genre that has intrigued me since I was an adolescent.

The editing and writing of new work required hours spent alone, a retreat. I stared at this green and gold world as I once stared at lizards darting into the shade, at desert willows in bloom, at dust devils spinning in the desert. When I looked out the windows of our third-floor apartment, I saw a cardinal graze wide leaves that spilled a glistening shower of rain. I stared in disbelief at the outrageous red feathers just as I stared at the raccoon who periodically watched me from atop a neighboring chimney, at fireflies blinking in the dark suggesting that fairies and elves might indeed hover in nearby bushes and shrubs.

On most such occasions of self-imposed solitude we're asking the persistent human question: Who am I? What have I learned in my years on this earth? The beginning of a decade, my distance from that spot on the U.S.-Mexican border where I had spent my life, the observance of the quincentenary, all presented an opportunity for pondering. This book is about the various threads of me, a Texican, as the writer Rolando Hinojosa-Smith calls those of us born in Texas of Mexican ancestry.

The land in the middle. "I am the middle woman, / not my mother, not my daughter."[2] I had at times considered *nepantla,* which means "place in the middle" in Nahuatl—one of Mexico's indigenous languages—as a possible title for a poetry collection. I may have first noticed the word in connection with Sor Juana Inés de la Cruz, the seventeenth-century author, Mexico's most acclaimed woman poet, who was born in San Miguel de Nepantla. Tonight I write these words from the middle of these United States, but I am a child of the border, that land corridor bordered by the two countries that have most influenced my perception of reality. In "Legal Alien" I wrote about the discomfort of "sliding back and forth / between the fringes of both worlds."[3] There probably isn't a week of my life that I don't have at least one experience when I feel that discomfort, the slight frown from someone that wordlessly asks, What is someone like her doing here? But I am in the middle of my life, and well know not only the pain but also the advantage of observing both sides, albeit with my biases, of moving through two, and, in fact, multiple spaces, and selecting from both what I want to make part of me, of consciously shaping my space.

Tonight my daughter Libby called, and I called my mother. Both are my good friends. I learn from the women who border me. The house you visit is in this middle land. Because of my years on a campus, I, like the Latinas on campuses today, live in the middle land between the university and the community, the Latino community, our broader civic community, and our international community.

I love words and their interweavings. I store them in the back of my head, in file boxes, in folders. I placed some of my favorite phrases and thoughts in a number of these rooms for your pleasure and pondering. I wanted to share many of the ideas and wordings I have saved, which have been part of me for years. It was impossible to identify all the sources for such quotations.

As you wander through these rooms, these essays, you will overhear quiet, intimate conversations with my family members in some. In others, you will hear many voices speaking, questioning our public discourse, affirming the right of Latinas and Latinos to be heard, to participate in shaping the future of this country. My life, like yours, includes these complexities. No one of us committed to social change lives a serene, lyrical life. You will wander out of the house at times and return to your life, to the personal and public voices of your world. I regret that we cannot meet personally when you finally close the door to this house. I would like to sit outside with you and hear your thoughts, since you will have taken the time to consider mine.

You will find yourself disoriented at times by the use of the word *we*. I know the feeling. I purposely let the meaning shift and slide as it does in my life. Who are the *we* of me? My family, writers, Chicanas, Southwesterners, mothers, women of color, daughters, Latinas, college graduates, Hispanas, wives, Mexicans, U.S. citizens, readers, advocates, Mexican Americans, women, educators, learners?

And the we of us is a problem. It was in the last decade that the government began using the label *Hispanic,* a term objectionable to some because it ignores our indigenous roots and was externally imposed. Are the 60 percent of us of Mexican descent Mexicans? Mexican Americans? Chicanas? These labels produce strong reactions. *Mexican American* is too moderate for some, *Chicana* too militant for others. Our labels continue to evolve. We cannot allow them to separate us and must grant one another the right to name ourselves. Given all that confronts us, we need to avoid the convenient trap of using linguistic debates to resist the discomfort of change, of learning to work with those who share our dissatisfaction with our cities, states, nation, the new world that is supposedly being ordered. I most often use the inclusive terms *Latina* and *Latino* in these essays because we—Puerto Ricans, Cubans, Mexican Americans, Central and South Americans—share if not fluency in the Spanish language, a respect for it, and values such as family and community. If we lack the courage to unite, we will diminish our power, the power to participate in creating a more just world.

Labels and labelers, the power of naming, do, of course, merit our scrutiny. Of all the bodies dwelling on the Americas, why are we The Americans? I blush at our persistent national arrogance. Even more embarrassing is that we believe our myth. *Siempre sigue la lucha*. The struggle continues, as my friend Rudy Anaya is fond of saying.

Each of us who raises her voice feels inadequate to counter the silence. The voices we hear and know merit so much more than we feel we can give. With particular poignancy we cry out with Borges, "Oh, incompetence." A cynic might say that we have been made to feel inadequate, never quite good enough, never bright or articulate enough, and that the resulting silence suits the dominating culture, intellectual oppression. But we write resisting internalized oppression, believing that the next generation will exceed us. While we struggle to discover our literary foremothers, perhaps if more of us write, new writers will see hope. Women and men of conscience do feed one another, sustain one another through faith, hope, courage. Certainly I have been nourished throughout my life by books and write, in part, to repay that debt.

In 1992 the Americas, in the appropriate rather than the appropriated sense of that word, is observing the quincentenary, the five-hundredth anniversary of *el encuentro,* "the encounter," between the Old and New worlds—again, the labeler defines perspective. New to whom? Initially this was to be a celebration of the discovery of America. Some balking ensued. "Celebrate imperialism and colonialism?" we asked, as did Mexico and other Latin American countries. "Discovery of a New World?" frowned descendants of the Maya, a civilization as complex as that of Mycenae. *Discovery* became *encounter,* illustrating the human struggle to clarify reality through language.

You will find, dear guest, that I bring more questions than answers, but they are questions too often ignored—about our economic, linguistic, and color hierarchies, about the power of naming in this country, about dominance and colonization, about unquestioned norms, about the need to create space for ourselves, individually and collectively.

The essays are about my encounters with my world, my attempt to clarify my musings through language, both Spanish and English. The essays competed with poems, family, friends, other work, and children's books; but near the end, a manuscript grips a writer by the throat. I completed the manuscript in the spring, a season of rebirth and renewal. Hope.

Notes

1. Pat Mora, "My Word-house," in *Communion* (Houston: Arte Público Press, 1991), p. 86.

2. Pat Mora, "It May Be Dangerous" (Unpublished poem).

3. Pat Mora, "Legal Alien," in *Chants* (Houston: Arte Público Press, 1984), p. 52.

2

THE BORDER

A Glare of Truth

I moved away for the first time from the U.S.-Mexican border in the fall of 1989. Friends were sure I'd miss the visible evidence of Mexico's proximity found in cities such as my native El Paso. Friends smiled that I'd soon be back for *good* Mexican food, for the delicate taste and smell of *cilantro,* for soft tortillas freshly made. There were jokes about care packages flying to the Midwest.

Although most of my adult home and work life had been spent speaking English, I was prepared to miss the sound of Spanish weaving in and out of my days like the warm aroma from a familiar bakery. I knew I'd miss the pleasure of moving back and forth between two languages—a pleasure that can deepen human understanding and increase our versatility conceptually as well as linguistically.

And indeed, when I hear a phrase in Spanish in a Cincinnati restaurant, my head turns quickly. I listen, silently wishing to be part of that other conversation, if only for a few moments, to feel Spanish in my mouth. I'm reading more poetry in Spanish, sometimes reading the lines aloud to myself, enjoying sounds I don't otherwise hear. Recently I heard a voice on National Public Radio say that learning another language is renaming

the world. What an interesting perception. Because language shapes as well as reflects our reality, exploring it allows us to see and to explore our world anew, much as experiencing the world with a young child causes us to pause, savor.

I smile when my children, who were too busy when they were younger, now inform me that when they visit they hope we'll be speaking Spanish. They have discovered as I did that languages are channels, sometimes to other people, sometimes to other views of the world, sometimes to other aspects of ourselves. So we struggle with irregular verbs, laughing together.

Is it my family—children, parents, siblings, niece, nephews —that I miss in this land of leaves so unlike my bare desert? Of course, but my family, although miles away, is with me daily. The huge telephone bills and the steady stream of letters and cards are a long-distance version of the web of caring we once created around kitchen tables. Our family web just happens to stretch across these United States, a sturdy, elastic web steadily maintained by each in his or her own way.

Oh, I miss the meals seasoned with that family phrase, "Remember the time when . . . ?" But I've learned through the years to cherish our gatherings when I'm in the thick of them, to sink into the faces and voices, to store the memories and stories like the industrious Ohio squirrel outside my window stores her treasures.

I've enjoyed this furry, scurrying companion as I've enjoyed the silence of bare tree limbs against an evening sky, updrafts of snow outside our third-floor window, the ivory light of cherry blossoms. I feel fortunate to be experiencing the geographical center of this country, which astutely calls itself the Heartland. If I'm hearing the "heart," its steady, predictable rhythms, what am I missing from this country's southern border, its margin?

Is it other rhythms? I remember my mixed feelings as a young girl whenever my father selected a Mexican station on the radio, feelings my children now experience about me. I wanted so to *be an American,* which in my mind, and perhaps in the minds of many on the border, meant (and means) shunning anything from Mexico.

But as I grew I learned to like dancing to those rhythms. I learned to value not only the rhythms but all that they symbolized. As an adult, such music became associated with celebrations and friends, with warmth and the sharing of emotions. I revel in a certain Mexican passion not for life or about life, but *in* life—a certain intensity in the daily living of it, a certain abandon in such music, in the hugs, sometimes in the anger. I miss the *chispas,* "sparks," that spring from the willingness, the habit, of allowing the inner self to burst through polite restraints. Sparks can be dangerous but, like risks, are necessary.

I brought cassettes of Mexican and Latin American music with us when we drove to Ohio. I'd roll the car window down and turn the volume up, taking a certain delight in sending such sounds like mischievous imps across fields and into trees. Broadcasting my culture, if you will.

Foreign Spooks

Released full blast into the autumn air
from trumpets, drums, flutes,
the sounds burst from my car like confetti
riding the first strong current.
The invisible imps from Peru, Spain,
Mexico grin as they spring from guitars,
harps, hand claps, and violins,
they stream across the flat fields of Ohio,
hide in the drafts of abandoned gray barns,
and the shutters of stern, white houses,

burrow into cold cow's ears and the crackle
of dry corn, in squirrel fur, pond ripple, tree gnarl,
owl hollow, until the wind sighs

and they open their wide, impudent
mouths, and together *con gusto*
startle sleeping farm wives,
sashaying raccoons, and even
the old harvest moon.[1]

On my first return visit to Texas, I stopped to hear a group
of *mariachis* playing their instruments with proud gusto. I was
surprised and probably embarrassed when my eyes filled with
tears not only at the music, but at the sight of wonderful Mexican faces. The musicians were playing for some senior citizens.
The sight of brown, knowing eyes that quickly accepted me
with a smile, the stories in those eyes and in the wrinkled faces
were more delicious than any *fajitas* or *flan*.

When I lived on the border, I had the privilege accorded to
a small percentage of our citizens: I daily saw the native land
of my grandparents. I grew up in the Chihuahua desert, as did
they, only we grew up on different sides of the Rio Grande.
That desert—its firmness, resilience, and fierceness, its whispered chants and tempestuous dance, its wisdom and majesty—
shaped us as geography always shapes its inhabitants. The desert
persists in me, both inspiring and compelling me to sing about
her and her people, their roots and blooms and thorns.

The desert is harsh, hard as life, no carpet of leaves cushions
a walk, no forest conceals the shacks on the other side of the sad
river. Although a Midwest winter is hard, it ends, melts into rich
soil yielding the yellow trumpeting of daffodils. But the desert
in any season can be relentless as poverty and hunger, reali-

ties prevalent as scorpions in that stark terrain. Anthropologist Renato Rosaldo, in his provocative challenge to his colleagues, *Culture and Truth*, states that we live in a world "saturated with inequality, power, and domination."[2]

The culture of the border illustrates this truth daily, glaringly. Children go to sleep hungry and stare at stores filled with toys they'll never touch, with books they'll never read. Oddly, I miss that clear view of the difference between my comfortable life and the lives of so many who also speak Spanish, value family, music, celebration. In a broader sense, I miss the visible reminder of the difference between my insulated, economically privileged life and the life of most of my fellow humans. What I miss about the sights and sounds of the border is, I've finally concluded, its stern honesty. The fierce light of that grand, wide Southwest sky not only filled me with energy, it revealed the glare of truth.

Notes

1. Pat Mora, "Foreign Spooks," in *Communion* (Houston: Arte Público Press, 1991), p. 24.
2. Renato Rosaldo, *Culture and Truth* (Boston: Beacon Press, 1989), p. 217.

ENDANGERED SPECIES

I've been eating strawberries. The juicy morsels remind me of a comment made by a colleague who had worked with senior citizens. They had firmly said to her: strawberries don't taste like they used to. Oh, they agreed that today's strawberries are larger, plumper, more uniform; but these veterans of many meals were convinced that the new hybrids lack the original, distinctive, deep red flavor. Nature thrives on variety, not monotony. Today's tall and flawless long-stemmed roses can likewise be beautiful to behold, but they lack the rich, heavy perfume of their less hybridized relatives. A common topic among those concerned with the natural world is the importance of genetic diversity, the risk of the current emphasis on a few high-yield species, the danger of hybridization. This phenomenon, of being seduced by the safety of uniformity, also confronts the Latino population and, in fact, all of us in this country. I write, in part, to resist that myth of safety.

I began making time for writing in about 1980. Like many Chicana writers, I was motivated to write because I felt our voices were absent from what is labeled American literature, but is U.S. Eurocentric literature seasoned sparingly with a bit of Color. Too often we are absent from classrooms, anthologies, bookstores. I advocated the preservation of our stories, songs, customs, and values in my writing, as do many of my fellow writers who were and are termed *ethnic writers,* a term that falsely suggests that some of us have ethnicity and some of us don't. At its most dangerous level, this label perpetuates the false notion that Anglo-American writers are the real writers, rather than one tradition in the evolving body of U.S. literature. My motivations to document, validate, and dignify were also those of my literary foremothers, as Tey Diana Rebolledo, Genaro Padilla, and other scholars who study the early writings of women of Mexican ancestry in this country remind me. I'm learning the names of these foremothers—Cleofas Jaramillo, who wrote *Romance of a Little Village Girl*; Fabiola Cabeza de Vaca, author of *We Fed Them Cactus.*

Although the genres to which I was initially drawn were poetry and children's books, I began to explore the essay because our media image, which emphasizes drugs, dropouts, delinquents, discouraged me. Little wonder some of our young people choose to minimize their cultural distinctiveness, part of their uniqueness. So often after a poetry reading or presentation in which I spoke about pride in Mexican heritage, parents would tell me that although they totally agreed with my comments, their children did not want to speak Spanish. They wanted to "blend in." These parents were often raised as I was, to value courtesy, warm interpersonal relationships, family, education. We were taught respect for authority and the importance of celebration, to listen to the elderly and delight in the newborn, to express our feelings: to laugh with enthusiasm, to cry with abandon, to take time with people. They feared these values were disappearing.

I responded that young people want to ally themselves with what their society values and rewards. James Baldwin, in his book *The Price of the Ticket*, writes of the psychic jolt when in our youth we realize that "the flag to which [we] have pledged allegiance has not pledged allegiance to [us]." We are shocked, he continues, to see ourselves rooting for heroes on the big screen even though they are killing people like us. Young people want to be part of a valued group, the perceived elite, and little they see in this media world suggests that Latinas and Latinos are creative or talented, that they thrive as leaders and thinkers and scientists and artists.

Today I invite these parents to stand back with me from our society and to see the patterns of dominance and repression, to explore the motivations for erasing languages and differences. Generalizations are difficult because cultures are neither static nor uniform, luckily. No race, sex, religion, or ethnic group can transform these United States, can whisper wisdom that will instantly cure our ills, but there has been a goal in this country to create a national culture. As literary critic Teresa McKenna states, this desire for a "common culture" is "based on obfuscation, cultural destruction and repression of difference."[1] We more critically need to examine issues of power and to engage our children and students in these discussions. We need to consider, for example, Professor Renato Rosaldo's intriguing notion of the inverse relationship between "full citizenship and cultural visibility."[2] Citizenship in the broadest terms, in the sense of full participation in the nation's public life, need not require melting in, shedding, or forgetting a part of ourselves. Citizenship should affirm, not deny, identity.

Change is occurring, but it is oh so slow. Some, although not enough of us, are now the directors, deans, managers, vice-presidents, and presidents of corporations and colleges. To what extent do we question and resist organizational and institutional practices that ignore the Latino community and its needs? To what extent do we struggle against inequities by effectively articulating needed change and transforming our professions through coalition building with ethical colleagues? Such struggles are exhausting. We need to support and encourage one another repeatedly, to ask the difficult and unwelcome questions about stereotypes, exclusion. How do we resist the rewards of betrayal? I am grateful for historian Juan Gómez-Quiñones's wisdom when he warns about the danger of equating a culture with tradition: "Returning to the source means not a recreating of the past but the building of the future: not to restore the past or to worship it as a false idol, but to build an authentic future, one which subsumes our past, not denies it."[3]

Just as there have been advocates of historical preservation and of natural conservation, individuals and groups who recognize that Williamsburg and whales are both worth preserving, there is a small cultural conservation movement in this country motivated by the conviction that we are all enriched by our unique cultural heritages, by our varying languages, traditions, and arts. (I sometimes joke that I'm not sure if this is a movement, because I have trouble finding anyone who has heard about it.) This country's conservationists urge us enthusiastically to protect and foster Navajo weaving, Cambodian dancing, black blues singing, *mariachi* music. They remind us that our pluralism enhances our group creativity, increases our options for expressing ourselves, enriches our lives.

We can take a leadership role in the cultural conservation movement. *Abuelas* (grandmothers) and *abuelos* (grandfathers) like mine were fiercely proud of their Mexican heritage and drew strength from their traditions. These grandparents and our parents are proud of our ability to speak English, to articulate the pain and sadness of discrimination, and to participate in the civic life of this country. Such skills, however, in no way require that we abandon our ability to speak Spanish, our belief in the importance of treating others with respect, our strong family ties. This concept of family needs to be expanded to include our national and international Latino community. *Tiene que ser una familia como las de nuestros antepasados: fuerte y cariñosa.* It needs to be a family that is like those of our ancestors: strong and affectionate.

Those old arguments that citizens must shed their language to "melt in" simply no longer apply. Many of us are not immigrants, and this is not a fledgling nation demanding uniformity for survival. Because as a country we have unfortunately adopted business metaphors to describe ourselves, the new global economy is sometimes used as a rationale for fluency in a number of languages. And indeed in this age of internationalization, as corporations and governments can attest, an understanding and appreciation of cultural differences is as essential a skill as technological competence. Certainly this country's flexibility is enhanced by having citizens of varied backgrounds who know, understand, and value their familial traditions, language, symbols, and yet are united by shared values such as the worth of each individual, the necessity of protecting basic human rights, and freedom of speech. Pragmatism, however, should be neither the only nor the primary motivation for valuing our distinctive group identities, our differences. This country has both the opportunity and the responsibility to demonstrate to this world of emerging representative governments that nurturing variety is central, not marginal, to democracy.

Special strategies will be needed to support and value ethnic diversity, rather than to deny or merely tolerate it, and Latinas should be involved locally and nationally, for collectively we can make a difference. In our universities and colleges, we can become more keenly aware of, and more aggressively question and resist, what critic Gloria Anzaldúa calls "the rhetoric of dominant ideology . . . [which] presents its conjectures as universal truths while concealing its patriarchal privilege and posture."[4]

How easy it is for us to be seduced by that myth of objectivity. Eloquently the myth is perpetuated at faculty meetings, at conferences, in journals: that thinking, writing, and speaking as *they* do, as European Americans do, constitutes excellence. "Oppressed groups are frequently placed in the situation of being listened to only if we frame our ideas in the language that is familiar to and comfortable for a dominant group," writes sociologist Patricia Hill Collins, author of *Black Feminist Thought*.[5]

We also can participate in our school districts, encouraging the selection of textbooks and programs that reflect the rich cultures present in this country, insisting that culture not be reduced to what anthropologist Louis Casagrande calls the "4F's": food, folklore, festivals, and fashion. Eating enchiladas in the cafeteria does not equal understanding Mexico. We can learn from the work of educators, such as Professor Eugene García, who study effective schools for our Latino communities, identity formation, and linguistic choice. We can learn more about programs such as the Kamehameha School in Hawaii, the Saturday Japanese schools, the inner-city schools that emphasize pride in African American heritage, the twenty-six American Indian colleges, the international schools, the Canadian Heritage Language Program. I look at an official poster printed in Canada that links the Canadian flag with "Multiculturalism and Citizenship Canada." Around a photograph of a dozen grinning youngsters of various ethnicities are the words, "Together We're Better! Let's Stop Racism." Where are our such national calls? Canada passed its Canadian Multiculturalism Act in 1988. A 1991 national survey mentioned in official Canadian brochures revealed that 77 percent of Canadians view diversity as characteristic of their country and as enriching it. Hmmm.

Aware of the value of family involvement in and support of the educational process, how will we engage parents and families, particularly those with limited or no English skills, those often made to feel unwelcome at our schools, libraries, museums, made to feel inferior? John Semuel, the head of the African National Congress' education department, talks about fostering a "culture of learning."[6] Because we know that expectation affects performance, this concept is also an important goal for Latinos, whether we are educators or not. We must look at who is staffing and who is leading our schools and broaden the definition of education to include an understanding and appreciation of the cultures that constitute our collective national heritage. I was surprised to note recently that although about one in four of us in this country identify ourselves as non-European, only 10 percent of the teachers and 8 percent of the student teachers are from the emerging majority.[7] How will we work with educational institutions to help them change from being threatening, judgmental environments to service entities preparing each youngster to think critically, to participate actively in a country of equally meritorious ethnicities?

We are one another's hope. I think of educators such as Josefina Tinajero, a professor of bilingual education and the editor of a bilingual reading series. When she began school in El Paso, she could speak no English. Like so many non-English-speaking youngsters, she could not communicate with her teacher, although she wanted to. She still saves the note written on her second grade report card: "Josefina needs to express herself in class and when she is playing with the other children." She tells me that she'd carefully memorize each spelling word, knowing she could do this, even though she had no idea what these words meant, nor did her parents. Remembering her pain clearly, and remembering the importance of her home environment, which valued knowledge and a command of Spanish, she now teaches teachers in Texas and throughout the country about the importance of interaction between reader and text, between a child and black marks on a page, between child and teacher.

I wonder why National Heritage Fellows, for example, and non–European American artists are not a more visible part of our national life, part of school children's educational experience. Since 1982 the National Endowment for the Arts through its Folk Arts Program has annually recognized traditional artists, weavers, storytellers, quilters, dancers. But the heroes and heroines of the young are often highly paid sports figures and music idols. Even in curriculum materials produced by school districts about "Hispanic Americans" it is media stars—actors and singers—rather than an acclaimed wood-carver or painter or novelist who is featured. Our cultural heritage needs to be part of our children's educational experience; it was not part of ours. Our cultures, our *common wealth,* are educational resources for the astute, concerned teacher. Just as we may best understand the structure and patterns of our native language when we explore a second language, perhaps we best begin to understand our own culture when we begin to study and understand the patterns and values of other groups. This journey is to be relished, not feared. What possibilities for making geography, history, and the arts more relevant, for encouraging U.S. youngsters to understand the meaning of global citizenship.

We can work with and in our day-care centers, libraries, and museums to foster programming and exhibits that include not only Western European traditions but a variety of cultures. At the national level, we can likewise support programs, publications, and the rare media ventures that increase our understanding and appreciation of the varied human groups on the planet, of their religions, music, science, customs. We also need to question and confront programs that ignore our presence and realities. We can encourage our youth, the next generation, to add their voices and talents to the richness of Latina traditions, our evolving collective consciousness. They need to know the work of visual artists such as Judith Baca, Rupert García, Ester Hernández, Luis Jiménez, and Carmen Lomas Garza. Cultural conservation does not seek merely to preserve the past but also to promote excitement about the evolution of cultural patterns, about current sculpture, writing, music—excitement about transformation.

We need to become much more aware of the homogenizing power of mass media, which effectively and cleverly convinces us to seek happiness by looking like a smiling, uniform model. Often the popular model has little to do with us. In our loud and brash society, our distinctiveness is steadily diminished through quiet losses: our children don't speak Spanish or kiss their elders on the cheek or listen patiently to *Abuelita*'s oft-repeated stories or question inequities. Like those perfect strawberries and uniform roses, Latinos will meet other's definitions of quality by settling for being mannequins, by losing the deep red flavor of our myths, music, values, Spanish—*nuestra sangre*.

I have more faith in these United States than those who shiver and shake that exploring our differences weakens us, who fear what some term our *Balkanization*. Weak and nervous families worry about a family member who doesn't fit the mold. Truly strong families broadcast the varying talents and perspectives of their members. To nurture Latina and Latino leaders in the next generation, we must ensure that our young people, and all young people, are taught not only by their families but also by their schools, communities, and the media to know their heritage, to be proud of what they are, to be inspired by their cultural past.

The ironies are always with us. A recent review of the book *Mystic Chords of Memory: The Transformation of Traditions in American Culture* by Michael Kammen mentions that after World War II, the inn at colonial Williamsburg did not welcome reservations by Jews and provided separate rest rooms for African Americans. So much for the rosy glow of preservation movements. Kammen's book also cautions against sacrificing historical accuracy to satisfy what he calls the "heritage syndrome," the desire for continuity in times of unrest.[8] At the same time that we question who determines accuracy, we need to resist believing only what is convenient and comforting.

I first heard the words *cultural conservation* at a 1987 conference in San Francisco entitled "From the Inside Out: Perspectives on Mexican and Mexican-American Folk Art." I will always be grateful for the fellowship that allowed me to attend that conference and discover cultural conservation. Learning about this effort to validate and cherish human expression helped me to speak more specifically about this topic as part of my poetry readings. I began to urge not only listeners of Mexican heritage but all listeners to explore and value their cultural background. Audiences respond positively to the notion, nod seeing the logic of valuing the myriad ways humans explain their world, how they celebrate, grieve. Obviously, I would be naïve and even foolish if I didn't realize the tangled underlying issues.

Among the many articulate speakers at the conference, I remember two good teachers who influenced my thinking, although I haven't seen them since—Archie Green, who was then Professor Emeritus at the University of Texas, and Lourdes Arizpe, who was the director of the National Museum of Popular Cultures in Mexico City. Archie spoke about the people who had been leaders in both the historic preservation and the natural conservation movements. His words were important because I knew absolutely nothing about the topic, but his enthusiasm and excitement about human ingenuity were even more important. He invited us to notice our surroundings, to be attentive, and to reflect on the particular craftsmanship of the ironworkers who years ago had constructed the room in which we sat. He spoke about the group's responsibility to be "cultural mediators, as teachers, as conveyers of tradition across ethnic lines, across economic lines, across social lines."

He made two observations that have stayed with me. He spoke about coalition building: how individual members of Congress had been engaged to focus on an area of agreement— in this case the preservation of traditional cultures—so necessary legislation, the American Folklife Preservation Act of 1976, would pass. I could just see him doing that, going office to office, grinning but determined, investing in producing change. He also said that the cultural conservation movement needed to study the natural conservation movement and learn from it. I would go further. Because humans are part of this natural world, we need to ensure that our unique expressions on this earth, whether art forms or languages, be a greater part of our national and international conservation effort.

Lourdes Arizpe reminded us that because we are a relatively new country, and a country obsessed with the new, we are not accustomed to discussing conservation. She helped me to become aware of questions that merit discussion: Why conserve? conserve what? how and for whom? and who should do the conserving?—questions still deserving more attention than they receive in cultural programming and in the often elitist world of museums. She reminded me of the importance of art for life's sake rather than for art's sake. She spoke about the "monetization" of art, of its becoming too expensive for its creators and about our tendency to put art under lock and key, in museums, to remove that beauty from everyday life. The artist affirms while she creates, and needs to better the world rather than being parted from it.

That conference in San Francisco was the beginning of my awareness that programs exist throughout the world to preserve and encourage the maintenance of cultural traditions. The National Museum of Folk Art and Traditions outside Paris is a premier example. The gallery guide begins with the words, "Every civilization, however humble it may be, manifests itself through two different aspects: on the one hand, it exists within the universe; on the other, it constitutes a universe, in itself." A notion worth pondering. I had been unaware that in this country, national and state programs to foster "folk life" exist, and unaware of the many debates, including the linguistic debates, about such terms. There was heated discussion at the conference as artists, historians, and anthropologists explored the complex issues of aesthetic standards, elite art, popular culture, and cultural equity. I was busy trying to sort through the ideas. I'm still sorting.

After the conference, and thanks to advice from anthropologist Alicia González at the Smithsonian, I visited the American Folklife Center at the Library of Congress, the Folklife Program at the Smithsonian, and the Folk Arts Program of the National Endowment for the Arts. I continue to learn about international conservation programs such as UNESCO's International Council on Monuments and Sites (ICOMOS), as well as to visit museums large and small everywhere I go. Reading publications produced by the national agencies, I wonder how aware even those of us in the Latino middle class are of the folklife programs in our own communities and regions, of the Annual Folklife Festival at the Smithsonian, and the annual naming of National Heritage Fellows: weavers, wood-carvers, dancers, fiddlers, potters, quilters, storytellers, mask makers— all artists who year after year perfect their traditional crafts. I study their faces in the January 1991 issue of *National Geographic*. I see George López, a ninety-year-old carver of *santos;* Juan Alindato, a Puerto Rican mask maker; Eppie Archuleta, a New Mexican weaver. Their faces glow with dedication. They remind me of George Bernard Shaw's belief that "this is the true joy in life, being used for a purpose recognized by yourself as a mighty one." How much they have to teach us about persistence and creativity. A Cajun fiddler says, "I'm watering the roots of this tree called Cajun culture so it can be preserved and grow."[9]

Where did the *chispas* come from? Why is *arte popular,* the term in Mexico for folk art, art of the people as opposed to what can be called elite or academic art, why is it one of the fires burning in some of us? There are psychological explanations, the longing for a quieter life, private inventiveness with a chosen medium, the interest in combining utility and beauty for a community by repeating a process that connects us to our ancestors. It is often more playful, takes itself less seriously. Among my personal explanations are my awe at the human ability, in the absence of physical comforts, to bring forth beauty. It's the shiver of delight when we see pansies in hard, cold ground, the blooms delicate in the snow. I think of the women I would see as a child at the *mercado* in Juárez. Their lives were not easy, but they would be laughing and talking to one another, calling out to prospective customers while their hands deftly turned paper into flowers.

Petals

have calloused her hands,
brightly-colored crepe paper: turquoise
yellow, magenta, which she shapes
into large blooms for bargain hunting tourists
who see her flowers, her puppets, her baskets,
but not her—small, gray-haired woman
wearing a white apron, who hides behind

blossoms in her stall at the market,
who sits and remembers collecting wildflowers
as a girl, climbing rocky Mexican hills
to fill a straw hat with soft blooms
which she'd stroke gently, over and over again
with her smooth fingertips.[10]

Although my life and the nature of my work separate me from being a traditional craftsperson, I want to learn from that world of women and men who have a strong sense of place, who daily work at their craft, choose a reliance on former community artists, seek to embed in their work patterns from the past, struggle and delight in bringing to those around them works of both use and beauty. Maya women weave designs that echo on cotton cloth, their white space; mine is paper.

Organizations such as Cultural Survival deal not with the pleasant and comforting aspects of fostering traditional culture, but with threatened, brutalized indigenous peoples throughout the world. Everywhere populations are at risk, in danger, endangered.

I read and save articles, reminders of the connection between cultural affirmation and mental health, such as women's cooperatives in Central and South America that confront societal ideology in the educational process, articles about those too-rare projects that value indigenous knowledge, that see it as a community and, in fact, a human resource. I keep articles about educators in India who struggle to introduce a curriculum that is Indian rather than European in its focus and examples about a United Nations educational project in Guatemala using native languages and reflecting community needs. Projects such as these—and Sna Jolobil, a weaving cooperative, and Sna Jtz'ibajom, a writing project, both in Chiapas— struggle to survive on meager funds. In this writing project,

Tzotzil and Tzeltal speakers collect and write the oral tradition that was being lost. Does a person have a basic right to her native language, culture? Can we imagine the impact if we or our children were denied that right? With enthusiasm the writers in Chiapas tell about the puppet shows they take to small villages high in the hills, sharing folktales and stories, weaving literacy efforts with cultural preservation, pride.

As we appropriately designate funds for the protection of animal and plant species, are we also designating funds to protect endangered peoples, their lifeways and languages? We read and hear statistics on plants and animals that will soon be extinct, but not about the disappearance of a language or art form or group. Is a language, that intricate human construct and all its music, its joy and lament, and all that it reveals about human ingenuity, of less value than the burning eyes of a large, magnificent cat? Why are we more moved by colorful birds and blooms than by people of Color? Are we preserving those endangered lush lands for those who live there or for ourselves? Peter Matthiessen, in an interview in connection with his book *African Silences*, said, "The great majority of Africans have never seen a lion. They're not allowed in their own parks, and they get no advantages from the wildlife or the tourist income."[11]

The questions being raised by Latina educators in this country are heard in many countries with a history of educational domination, and the unnoticed struggle to assist groups to survive and to maintain their cultural identity has implications for the Latino population in the United States. In the closing address of the Smithsonian conference entitled "Why Preserve the Past? The Challenge of Our Cultural Heritage," the former director general of UNESCO, Amadou-Mahtar M'Bow, noted that "conservation of the past cannot simply be an end in itself; it must also contribute to the task of shaping the future by providing children and adults—*all* children and *all* adults—

with educational and training opportunities that foster personal development as well as the advancement of their societies." [12]

What writer Audre Lorde says to black men and women is true for all of us: "If we do not define ourselves for ourselves, we will be defined by others—for their use and to our detriment." [13] Our country and perhaps all human history is a pattern of oppression, repression, suppression, subjugation. Racism is part of our heritage, reminding us that not all aspects of a culture should be preserved. Regrettably, within individual cultures patterns of discrimination continue, whether based on gender, class, physical abilities, age, sexual preference, or religion. In part what we need, in Herbert Schiller's words, is "a principle of resistance—the reinterpretation of history, from a class perspective, made widely accessible to the people." [14] And even the word *preservation* connotes formaldehyde, of a suffocating and stifling of growth and change when indeed a true ethic of conservation includes a commitment to a group's decisions, its development and self-direction.

Complex. As a country we seem to get a certain thrill—and, in fact, invest billions—storming someone else's desert; we invest a small amount to preserve endangered species—plants and animals though seldom threatened peoples, their languages, or traditions; we invest an even smaller amount to encourage cultural expressions in public spaces; we remain nervous about investing significantly in the education of young people who don't really "look American." How do we ensure that the conservation and interest in "expressive culture" is not merely an interest in objects or art forms, art for art's sake in the area of popular culture, but that the basis of the conservation effort is a belief in the dignity of the individual, in true cultural equity—linguistic, artistic, civic? Because we are an industrialized nation, we often value products more than people. We reduce cultures to objects and welcome the objects but not the makers into our living rooms. By imposing our aesthetics on the economically dependent, we "commodify" cultures for our consumption. Even our discussions about appropriate language are difficult. Terms such as *folk art* remain controversial. Our linguistic discussions and debate reveal our national unease about who we are and about who has the power of naming.

Is the U.S. economic system our problem? We, Latinas and Latinos, need to become more vocal about our group heritage and more critical of the values of consumerism, violence, and social stratification that arrive silently in our mailboxes and appear almost every place we look. Sorely missed writer and university president Tomás Rivera told us that Chicano academics and the Chicano community needed to work together to "develop, as a priority, a *civic morality . . . Ni mas, ni menos.*"[15] We need to be more inquisitive, inquisitive about who controls our highly centralized media—what we see in movies, newspapers, and magazines, on billboards and movie screens. Who shapes our economic and educational policy? Who shapes our curricula and museum exhibits? Who leads the cultural conservation efforts in our country and in our states? Who is ensuring that the history of Latinas and Latinos in this country is being accurately and compellingly taught and that our present artists, whether in traditional or emerging art forms, are receiving a just portion of both the public and private support available? Who determines our aesthetic standards? Ethnomusicologist Alan Lomax, who, among others, has written about the implications of our highly centralized communications system, uses the label *aesthetic imperialism* to describe the Western European tradition of music education,[16] the steady devaluing of native sounds and rhythms. Certainly the term is also applicable to the arts and art education in general in this and any country with a history of colonization. Lomax calls this a "degradation" of our human culture and a "threat to the human imagination and to human variety." [17]

Individually we need to become more aware of the truth of Rosaldo's words, "Even when they appear most subjective, thought and feeling are always culturally shaped and influenced by one's biography, social situation, and historical context." [18]

Demographers predict that Latinos will be this nation's largest non-Anglo group at about the turn of the century. And yet we often remain invisible in the life of these United States, unless the news is bad news—crime, poverty. I keep looking for us when I go through what the mail brings, but I don't see us. With Arturo Madrid we know how it feels to be "a missing person." [19] I don't see us leading the country politically or economically. I don't see us directing or starring in major movies or television programs. I don't see us leading foundations or national non-Latino organizations. I don't see our pictures or names in the prestigious daily or monthly publications. I rarely see us receiving Pulitzers, Guggenheims, MacArthurs, NEA or NEH grants.

I continue to despair at how invisible U.S.-born Latinas and Latinos remain on the literary landscape. I want to believe with professor and editor Charles Tatum that, like African American literature, Chicano literature has, or soon will have, "the same legitimate place in the American social, cultural, and literary mainstream." [20] Editors such as Tatum, Nicolás Kanellos, Gloria Anzaldúa, Tey Diana Rebolledo, Gary Keller, and Ray González, among others, labor to anthologize and publish our work. But I still think that most of the well-known Latino literary names are foreign. I too eagerly read Allende, Márquez, Fuentes, Paz, but can it be that there are no eloquent or moving native U.S. Latina and Latino writers? Wander major bookstores and try to find us. Major publishers and editors continue this country's historical pattern of affirmative action: affirming that men of Western European ancestry are better—they are the critical thinkers, the effective leaders, the inspired artists. Our absence means that our voices—the stories, anger, fears, and hope of our national community, remain unheard and thus comfortably ignored. We have a long way to go.

I don't see us published by major publishing companies, but then we are not editors of major presses or publications. I don't see us teaching at major writing conferences or reading in major reading series. I don't see us among the speakers and readers at the International Reading Association or the Society of Children's Book Writers. Is it really that our work is inferior, that *we* are inferior? Or is it that not enough of us are part of committees and meetings, often secret, "No applications accepted"?

Few of us have had bicoastal educational training; we don't have bicoastal networks. We are outsiders to the power systems, whether political, economic, educational, scientific, artistic. Why is it preposterous to imagine a Chicana as president of the United States? This is the country in which anyone can be president, right? Ah, *Virginia,* that would be right.

Some of us wish to separate ourselves from such predictable systems of discrimination, but others want the national life of this country to include us. We want to see Latinas and Latinos who are committed to our national community and to social equity as leaders in politics, education, health, research, the arts.

The 1991 winner of the Nobel Peace Prize, Aung San Suu Kyi, writes, "It is not power that corrupts but fear."[21] In continuing house arrest in her own country, she knows too well about physically repressive regimes. But her interesting statement has implications for our daily lives. Those who have any degree of power fear losing the bit we have and struggle to hold on to it. Also, we fear the unending confrontations necessary to insist on greater equity for those who speak no English, who can't afford adequate housing and health care, who are illiterate, who are physically abused, who are unwelcome at our educational institutions, who do not receive major posts and awards not because they lack potential or skills or talent, but because they are different, because they do not conform to a white, elitist, class-exclusionary, unstated norm.

How can I be a child of the border and not know with Audre Lorde that in this country "oppression is as american as apple pie."[22] But the colonizer's mentality—and rewards—exist worldwide. The same linguistically repressive tactics have been used on the Maya in Mexico by their Spanish-speaking teachers as have been used in this country. My Guatemalan friend Don Fernando Tesucún, who does restoration work at the site of Tikál, tells me, "When I was a little boy, the teachers at my school would hover just waiting to hear me whisper to my friends in my Maya language so that they could whip me for not speaking Spanish." The dominant society in this country is not the only group guilty of such psychological brutality. Evil, like talent, intelligence, and creativity, is not genetically linked to skin color. History, pernicious patterns of entitlement, human greed, fear, societal values—all contribute to a reluctance to demand change—in ourselves, and then in our communities. Persistence is often rewarded. Today Don Fernando is assisting anthropologists to prepare a written record of his language, Itza Maya, the language he refused to relinquish.

The Talmud says, "It is not incumbent upon thee to complete the task but neither are thou free to desist from thy part." Those of us committed to social change struggle together, some as critics of this society, some as teachers, labor organizers, nurse's aides, office workers, cooks, artists, politicians, concerned parents. Our increased awareness and participation in cultural conservation efforts and opportunities can help shape how and what our children learn about their heritage and heritages. As educator Rosalinda Barrera writes, much of the children's literature about us is written by Anglos and usually describes us "through limited, distorted, and negative portrayals." The writing "reveals more about the dominant society's attitudes and thoughts about Mexican Americans at a particular time than it does about the Mexican American experience itself."[23]

A key impetus for me in this conservation work is that we know the psychological value of ethnic pride. Studies, such as the 1990 report on "Ethnic Images" by the University of Chicago's Opinion Research Center, sadly remind us that we are far from "approaching a color and creed-blind society."[24] Latina and Latino youngsters, and all youngsters, need and deserve day-care centers, schools, textbooks, libraries, museums, artistic performances, books, movies, and television programs that reflect the cultural backgrounds served. Although I understand the impetus for separatist schools and support the concept on an experimental basis in these troubled times, I hope for truly integrated public educational opportunities that will help young people know and share their heritages—Mexican, Polish, Chinese, African, Indian. We can prepare young people for living with prejudice so that they are not totally devastated by it. They need to know that it exists, and they need specific knowledge of their heritage for "resistance and affirmation." (What fine coupling of those words and concepts in the title of a recent major art exhibit: "CARA, Chicano Art: Resistance and Affirmation.") Our youth need to see their parents and teachers, their role models, participating in public discourse and actively participating in their societies, so that they, the next generation, will do likewise.

Obviously, one can be cynical about conservation efforts, but the present and future generations of Mexican American youngsters can thrive in a more conducive and respectful environment if we participate, actively participate, in shaping the educational institutions, cities, states, and nation in which these young women and men will develop. "Every child has a right to be cherished," a poster says. Every child and person also has a right to have what she *is* cherished—the color of her skin, the texture of his hair. My investment is in the future. I suppose that is one of the many reasons why I write children's books.

Pride in cultural identity, in the set of learned and shared language, symbols, and meanings, needs to be fostered not because of nostalgia or romanticism, but because it is essential to our survival. The oppressive homogenization of humanity in our era of international technological and economic interdependence endangers us all. New Mexican *santero* George López says about his carving, "It's in the blood. It's part of my name."[25] Ethnic groups are this nation's blood. We all need more boldly to be part of its name.

Notes

1. Teresa McKenna, "Establishing Equilibrium: Diversity in the Curriculum." (Paper presented at the symposium on "Diversity, the Curriculum, and the Classroom," sponsored by the Provost and Center for Excellence in Teaching, University of Southern California, Los Angeles, November 6, 1991), p. 2.

2. Renato Rosaldo, *Culture and Truth* (Boston: Beacon Press, 1989), p. 198.

3. Juan Gómez-Quiñones, *On Culture*, UCLA–Chicano Studies Center Publications, Popular Series no. 1 (Los Angeles, 1977), p. 21.

4. Gloria Anzaldúa, *"Haciendo caras, una entrada,"* *Making Face, Making Soul: Haciendo Caras*, ed. Gloria Anzaldúa (San Francisco: Aunt Lute Foundation, 1990), p. xxiii.

5. Patricia Hill Collins, *Black Feminist Thought* (New York: Routledge, 1990), p. xiii.

6. Linda Vergani, "Anti-Apartheid Groups Hope to Map Future of Education in South Africa," *Chronicle of Higher Education*, 12 February 1992, p. A43.

7. Susan Chira, "Efforts to Reshape Teaching Focus on Finding New Talent," *New York Times*, 28 August 1990, p. B-5.

8. Mary Warner Marien, review of *Mystic Chords of Memory: The Transformation of Tradition in American Culture*, by Michael Kammen, *Christian Science Monitor*, 16 January 1992, p. 13.

9. Marjorie Hunt and Boris Weintraub, "Masters of Traditional Arts," *National Geographic*, January 1991, p. 75.

10. Pat Mora, "Petals," in *Chants* (Houston: Arte Público Press, 1984), p. 29.

11. Peter Matthiessen, interview in *New York Times Book Review*, 18 August 1991, p. 3.

12. Amadou-Mahtar M'Bow, "Closing Address to a Conference on Cultural Preservation," in *The Challenge to Our Cultural Heritage: Why Preserve the Past* (Washington, D.C.: Smithsonian/UNESCO, 1986), p. 234.

13. Audre Lorde, *Sister Outsider* (Freedom, Calif.: The Crossing Press, 1984), p. 45.

14. Herbert Schiller, *Communication and Cultural Domination* (Armonk, N. Y.: M. E. Sharpe, 1976), p. 88.

15. Tomás Rivera, "The Role of the Chicano Academic and the Chicano Non-academic Community," in *Tomás Rivera 1935–1984: The Man and His Work*, ed. Lattin, Hinojosa, and Keller (Tempe, Ariz.: Bilingual/Review Press, 1988), p. 43.

16. Alan Lomax, "Appeal for Cultural Equity," *Journal of Communication* 27, no. 2 (Spring 1977) p. 128.

17. Lomax, "Appeal for Cultural Equity," pp. 127, 138.

18. Rosaldo, *Culture and Truth*, p. 103.

19. Arturo Madrid, "Diversity and Its Discontents" (Claremont, Calif.: Tomás Rivera Center, 1988), p. 1.

20. Charles M. Tatum, ed., *New Chicana/Chicano Writing* (Tucson: University of Arizona Press, 1992), p. xi.

21. Takashi Oka, "Crusader for Democracy," *Christian Science Monitor*, 10 December 1991, p. 13.

22. Lorde, *Sister Outsider*, p. 10.

23. Rosalinda B. Barrera, "The Mexican American Experience in Children's Literature: Past, Present, Future," *Oregon English Journal*, vol. xiv, no. 1, Spring, 1992, pp. 12–13.

24. Tom Smith, "Ethnic Images," National Opinion Research Center, GSS Topical Report no. 19 (Chicago: University of Chicago, 1990), p. 4.

25. Hunt and Weintraub, "Masters of Traditional Arts," p. 77.

4

USED FURNITURE

A pre-Columbian epic poem says,

> Also they grew cotton
> of many colors:
> red, yellow, pink,
> purple, green, bluish-green,
> blue, light green
> orange, brown, and dark gold.
> These were the colors of the cotton itself.
> It grew that way from the earth,
> no one colored it.[1]

The images are rich, a legacy to be valued. The poet Anne Sexton writes, "The writer is essentially a crook / Out of used furniture he makes a tree."[2] As a writer I am most selfishly committed to retrieving my Mexican past because I want all that wonderful used furniture. Whether the artifacts are potsherds or myths, they enrich the well from which I draw. The notion of the creative unconscious is most intriguing in the specific. As a writer of Mexican heritage, I want to know about the indigenous peoples in Mexico's history and Mexico's present, about the Toltecs of old as well as the Tarahumaras of today. Their incantations, customs, myths are like discovering strands dyed to a rich hue with natural substances—berries, blossoms, bark—strands that I can then weave into my images, making them distinctive from writers of other ethnic backgrounds, adding a dimension to our collective offering.

I want to hear that which is part of me but which was silenced through both ignorance and prejudice. And I not only want to hear the voices; I want to be one of the women who writes the voices, "to trap / them on my cloth with a web of thin threads,"[3] that they may live on. My hope is that of Argentina's Luisa Valenzuela, that "with luck, something will be said through me, despite myself."[4] The heavy self. Perhaps this is one way of putting my privileges—health, education, physical comforts—to use.

Like many Latinas in this country, I was educated with few if any references to my Mexican American history, to part of my literary and human heritage. I was a university administrator attending a conference on the future of women's education at Stephens College in Columbia, Missouri, before I heard and heeded the concept that minorities are often educated away from themselves. Stephens, the kind of institution about which I knew nothing, was celebrating its 150th anniversary with a meeting entitled "All of Us Are Present." There was a certain irony in the title that might have been lost on me at the time. There was, I believe, only one other Chicana there. No Latina was even part of the program. How I leaned forward in my seat when, in a question and answer session, a woman at the microphone mentioned *pan dulce*.

I found Rusty Barcelo later, a wonderful Chicana administrator working steadily for students in Iowa. Meeting her was a benefit of the conference, as were the presentations and proceedings, all the ideas, and even the experience of again being invisible in a gathering that had inclusiveness as part of its focus. I get comfortable in my protected life. Feeling excluded reminded me of how often we diminish others by omitting them from our circle because their skin is too light or too dark, because their accent is not European or too European, because they have or lack doctorates or publications, because they went to the wrong schools or didn't go to school, because they are too political or not political enough, because their palms are too smooth or too rough, because they are not *us* and not among those we have chosen to receive our approval and attention. The challenge, of course, is to develop the habit of often glancing out of the corner of our eye for the forgotten.

Like many, I continue to ponder what it means that all of us in this country have been educated with only a Eurocentric aesthetic. Wordsworth, Whitman, and Dickinson were the poets I was asked to memorize. I will always love them, but how I regret that I lived for years without the sounds of Lorca (*"La guitarra / hace llorar a los sueños"*)[5] and Neruda (*"De tanto amor mi vida se tiñó de violeta"*)[6] moving in me. When I attended that conference in Missouri, I was already spending more and more time listening to words talk to one another, as Frost says. The more I spent time writing, the more my desire to educate myself beyond the rich stories my *tía* told me increased.

I began to collect more books about Mexico and about Mexican Americans, to discover images, stories, and rhythms that I wanted to incorporate. Obviously I learned more about Mexico's grandeur and conquest and also about contemporary problems, unresolved issues of land use, lack of health care and social services, political corruption, comfort for the few at the expense of the many, fierce discrimination against indigenous people. Our issues also; not lyrical topics, but realities cold and hard as the earth in a winter storm.

It had been easy to ignore Mexico as a source of creativity

on the border because it is often treated as inferior and because it is so familiar. Mexico was like a beautiful chest of smooth, dark wood that my mother had in her bedroom. I think she even called it her hope chest. I walked by the chest for years, probably had even watched my mother open it without paying much attention. Then one day, I really noticed, saw it. I opened the long lid and began to study the interior and to be fascinated by what it held of my family's past—special clothes wrapped in the rustle of tissue paper, my face in black and white grinning from a valentine I'd made in the first grade, romantic cards from my father to my mother. I had been ignoring treasures.

Life is like that, private awakenings that lead us to ask ourselves, Where have I been? Why haven't I noticed? I experienced that not uncommon transformation experienced by many whose pasts have been ignored or diminished: I began to see Mexico, to see its people, hear its echoes, gaze up at its silent and silenced grandeur. My Mexicanness became a source of pride. I had grown up in an environment that did not value, and often hated, my cultural heritage. Those in positions of power, the audible voices of political, educational, cultural, and economic leaders tried, some still try, to ignore or suppress— dark skin, the Spanish language, expressiveness. I, like so many other dwellers in that Southwestern desert, grew up ambivalent. Being "American" was and is given great importance. Now some of us realize that America is a continent and not a country. We are becoming less chauvinistic and beginning to speak of U.S. natives, U.S. English, U.S. literature.

I and my fellow Chicanas enjoy a cultural dual citizenship in two of the continent's countries. Critic Gloria Anzaldúa astutely assists us to see the strength of being *la mestiza,*[7] the strength of seizing the richness of the cultures that are our inheritance: indigenous, Spanish, and their mix: Mexico; and these United States: our mix. Like the feathered serpent of Mexico's my-thology, a creature that could move between two realms, earth and sky, we also exist in duality. My personal experience with internalized racism helps me to be patient and hopeful for the young who may feel as I did. Youngsters yearn for approval because their self-doubt is so immense. They long to belong, to be like the smiling images they see on screen after screen. And we—the brown-skinned—are usually screened out, except when the news is bad news.

Why do I seek to incorporate Latin American and particularly Mexican voices into myself? I was invited to mull the question over by anthropologist José Limón, who organized a panel for the Modern Language Association on "Retrieving Our Past, Determining Our Future." I sat and asked myself why so many writers and educators study the countries in which our grandparents took their first breath, their first steps, or study our people's ways in foreign or invaded soils. In part, we are affirming that they are part of us and that we are part of them. We seek to honor them, to hold on to what they created. I think of Manuel de Falla and Federico García Lorca, creatures of enormous creativity, working to preserve their Andalusian tradition of *el canto hondo,* "the deep song." Uruguayan writer Eduardo Galeano says, "Our authentic collective identity is born out of the past and is nourished by it . . . but this identity is not frozen into nostalgia."[8] As humans we are often fleeing, or at least taking halting steps, from isolation. Though in our noisy world solitude may have a sweet appeal, we know we are social creatures often driven to diminish our aloneness by relationships—ties with family or friends, professional memberships, belonging to what we might view as a cadre of true writers or scholars. We are also intrigued by our cultural past for a sense of definition in our chosen area of work, as well as for a sense of participation in a tradition, becoming part of a process we hold dear; be it historical research, folktale analysis, the documentation of oral history, poetry. We are psychologically comforted by being part of a continuum—diminished isolation, if you will—at the intellectual level. Writers in a particular way need this companionship of voices from the past, for our work is solitary. By ourselves, we seek to put ourselves, in the words of photographer André Breton, "in a state of grace with chance, so that something might happen, so that some one might drop in."

Readers, both student and nonstudent, also crave knowledge of their past, particularly when they begin to sense how much they don't know. Certainly after the upheavals of the sixties, some faculty members and the directors of Chicano studies programs and Latin American programs were aware of their hunger and the hunger of their students for the echoes from the past. "Turning inward to explore, decipher, and interpret elements from the Chicano cultural matrix, artists and intellectuals found strength and recovered meaning in the layers of everyday life practices," writes art critic Tomás Ybarra-Frausto.[9] Small presses struggled and continue to struggle to survive and meet this need. Chicana and Latino professors developed and develop course outlines and seminars on Chicano politics, border history, Latin American politics, Chicana literature. Certainly the oral tradition, an experience most of us treasure, is a persistent element in this process. Rather than being the subject of history, some of us now write it. "Each generation interprets the past in a different light with a different purpose," says Robert Pastor in *Limits of Friendship*.[10] Historians Vickie Ruiz, Oscar Martínez, Emma Pérez, and Mario García, among many others, document our past, the usually untold facts and stories. There also has been a political, or populist, vein, writings of social protest describing economic exploitation, blatant discrimination. The mere title of Lorna Dee Cervantes's "Poem for the Young White Man Who Asked Me How I, an Intelligent, Well-Read Person Could Believe in the War Between Races" suggests her perspective.

> I am not a revolutionary,
> I don't even like political poems.
> Do you think I can believe in a war between races?
> I can deny it. I can forget about it
> when I'm safe,
> living on my own continent of harmony
> and home, but I'm not
> there.[11]

As with any group, there is diversity within it. Some Latina and Latino writers write in Spanish, some in English, some use code-switching. Many use informal linguistic patterns, whereas others are movingly lyrical. Although there are considerable stylistic differences and few Chicana writers are products of formal writing programs, there is the determination to be accessible to our primary audience. Thus although convoluted poetry may be in vogue in some circles, many Latino writers value clarity. We are often discouraged that major presses and anthologies ignore us, but we find solace in what John Updike calls, "Singing the hitherto unsung."

Concerned educators dissatisfied with excluding the breadth and depth of this country's native voices are becoming familiar with our writing. They listen to what it says, assign it, insist that new and traditional anthologies include it, invite us to their readings. Colleges and universities are beginning to hire us as visiting writers, but more of us need to be in tenured positions. We need to be valued for what we are, supported to perfect our craft, be it research or creative writing, valued for our difference. Colleges and universities concerned about the education of their students need us to thrive in their faculties, on their campuses.

The future work for those of us whose ancestors spoke Spanish? Much to be done. We desperately need nationally recognized leaders and role models; we need to increase political participation, to demand that educational institutions address our needs as creatively as advertisers address our buying potential. We need children's books that describe the strength and variety of our homes and families; we need our fiction, poems, and essays in school texts, on college reading lists and in people's living rooms. We, and our children, need and deserve our history, which includes our artistic history. We also, like all humans, deserve the right to be ourselves, our complex selves. Because so few U.S.-native Latino writers are published, we become representatives of our group. This honors us. A few editors and arts administrators are making an effort to include women and Latinos, and it's flattering to be invited to give readings or to be included in textbooks and anthologies. My ego is one of the standard variety, voracious. I often tease organizers of panels or readings in the Midwest that just by walking in I fill two of their diversity slots—woman and Latina. But I think that each of us committed to having the Latina voice heard and valued in this country want, as Sandra Cisneros often says, to be one of many voices and not *the* voice, for we know the grand variety in our community, *and we want others to recognize this human wealth*. We encourage those who hear us or read us to become familiar with the many and varied Latina voices, for ultimately each of us knows that we can only speak for ourselves. In one of his last public lectures, another El Paso writer, Stanford professor Arturo Islas, said what we've all felt: "The whole question of who or what a writer 'represents' seems always to come back to my own heart and not anyone else's." [12]

Ethnic groups *are* different, thank God. And increasingly this nation is exploring the implications of the differences, recognizing that cultural and linguistic pluralism offers hope for shattering shackling stereotypes, for nurturing cultural vitality. Obviously such efforts are not a panacea for our many national woes. Complex problems require complex responses, but people need our assistance to maintain and explore their native language and customs, and we must accord such variety our attention and respect. Preserving language and rituals has historical relevance and psychological significance, because customs provide a context, allowing us to better understand political, and even educational, trends. Retrieving the past is historically sound, politically expedient, psychologically healthy, linguistically necessary, morally essential.

Assisting in the retrieval of our cultural past and that of those around us is a quiet form of rebellion. As moviemakers and television producers, advertisers and politicians bombard us with their versions of what we were, what we are, and what we want, we can continue to educate ourselves about the accurate record of our peoples. How dull to think that there is only one American dream, that regardless of color or race, we all want small nuclear families that have Porsches and pools, that look eternally young, whose sex drives, if harnessed, could heat a major metropolitan metroplex.

We are beings with ancestors who fought and wept and laughed and sang. We struggle to hear them, to tell their tales— yes, to diminish our isolation; yes, to enrich the lives of our fellow citizens; yes, to provide us worn furniture for creating trees. As humanists we should revere the human past and present as much as ecologists revere the land—as enlightening, intriguing, relevant. We are the one species that can derive strength and solace from communicating its myths, legends, poems. By listening to the varying versions we can smile, nod, delight in the unique, yet see, really see, the deep, persistent human truths, see beyond the grievance to the grief.

Notes

1. Miguel León-Portilla, *Pre-Columbian Literatures of Mexico* (Norman: University of Oklahoma Press, 1975), p. 41.

2. Maxine Kumin, *To Make a Prairie: Essays on Poets, Poetry, and Country Living* (Ann Arbor: University of Michigan Press, 1979), p. 25.

3. Pat Mora, "Bribe," in *Chants* (Houston: Arte Público Press, 1991), p. 7.

4. Luisa Valenzuela, "Writing with the Body," in *The Writer on Her Work: New Essays in New Territory*, ed. Janet Sternberg (New York: W. W. Norton, 1991), p. 199.

5. "The guitar / makes dreams weep." Federico García Lorca, *Poem of the Deep Song: Poema del cante jondo* (San Francisco: City Lights Books, 1931), p. 60.

6. "By so much love my life was tinted purple." Pablo Neruda, *100 Love Sonnets: Cien sonetas de amor* (Austin: University of Texas Press, 1959), p. 136.

7. Gloria Anzaldúa, "*La conciencia de la mestiza:* Towards a New Consciousness," in *Making Face, Making Soul: Haciendo Caras*, ed. Gloria Anzaldúa (San Francisco: Aunt Lute Foundation, 1990), pp. 377–89.

8. Eduardo Galeano, "In Defense of the Word," in *Multi-cultural Literacy*, ed. Rick Simonson and Scott Walker (St. Paul: Graywolf Press, 1988), p. 121.

9. Tomás Ybarra-Frausto, "Rasquachismo: A Chicano Sensibility," in *Chicano Art: Resistance and Affirmation, 1965–1985* (Los Angeles: Frederick S. Wight Art Gallery, Up. niversity of California, 1991), p. 159.

10. Robert A. Pastor and Jorge Castañeda, *Limits to Friendship: The United States and Mexico* (New York: Vintage Books, 1988), p. 45.

11. Lorna Dee Cervantes, "Poem for the Young White Man Who Asked Me How I, an Intelligent, Well-Read Person Could Believe in the War Between Races," in *Emplumada* (Pittsburgh: University of Pittsburgh Press, 1981), p. 35.

12. Arturo Islas, "On the Bridge, at the Border: Migrants and Immigrants," Ernesto Galarza Commemorative Lecture, Stanford Center for Chicano Research, 1990, p. 2.

5

For a Southwesterner, early spring in the Midwest is a time for
jubilation. Another winter survived. Why, then, on a soft spring
Saturday would I choose to leave the dogwoods and daffodils
and spend my day inside museums?

Certainly I didn't spend my youth enduring trips through
solemn rooms being introduced to "culture." There was only
one small art museum in my home town, and I'm not sure
how comfortable my parents would have felt there. My father
worked evenings and weekends to support the four of us and
to give us what he and my mother hadn't had, a youth without
financial worries. And my mother not only helped him in his
optical business but also was our willing chauffeur, in addition
to assisting the grandmother and aunt who lived with us.

But as an adult I began to visit these echoing buildings. A
fellowship allowed trips to modest and grand museums in New
York, Paris, Washington, Mexico, Peru, Hawaii, the Dominican Republic. And much to my surprise, I even found myself
directing a small university museum for a time, having the opportunity to convince people of all ages and backgrounds that
indeed the museum was theirs. I was hooked for life.

For me, museums are pleasure havens. When I enter, my

breathing changes just as it does when I visit aquariums, zoos, botanical gardens. These latter sites offer a startling array of living species. Unless we have become totally desensitized to nature's grandeur, to its infinite variations, arboretums and nature centers inspire us to treat our earth with more care, to be more attentive to the life around us no matter how minute, to notice. Like my son, Bill, I stand entranced by the spriteliness of glass shrimp, the plushness of the jaguar, the haughtiness of birds of paradise in bloom. Parrots make me laugh, fins spin my blood, ferns hush my doubts. I leave refreshed.

When they were younger, my children could far more easily understand my desire to visit displays of living creatures than they could my penchant for natural history and art museums, for gazing at baskets and pottery, at sculpture and flashing neon. It sounded like work walking through room after room, up and down stairs, being relatively quiet, not eating, reading small cards of text, staring at "weird" objects. This is fun?

But museums remind me of the strength and inventiveness of the human imagination. They remind me that offering beauty to a community is a human habit, a needed reminder in a society with little time for observing, listening, appreciating. I gaze at African masks crusted with cowrie shells, at drums and carvings of old, wrinkled wood, at the serenity of Buddha. I watch my fellow visitors drawn to cases both by the beauty and craft, but also as a kind of testimony to humans who once sat under our sun and moon and with rough hands graced our world.

I walk on and see the sturdy pre-Columbian female figures from Nayarit, Mexico, women of broad dimensions who occupy space rather than shrinking as we sometimes do. I see pan pipes and bone flutes from Peru, 180 B.C., back then, high in the Andes, hear a man transforming his breath into music.

Room after room I watch light and shadow play on sandstone, silver, wood, bronze, earthenware, copper, ivory, hemp, oil, acrylic, watercolor, straw, gold. I study toenails on a headless marble statue, watch light stroke the soft curves, wish I could touch her outstretched Roman hand. The next room, or turning a corner, can yield surprise, the halls and rooms a pleasure maze. I stand in Chagall's blue light, see his glass bird poised to fly from room to room.

I ignore the careful museum maps, enjoying the unexpected, the independence of viewing at will, the private pleasure of letting myself abandon order and logic room to room. Purposeless wandering? Not really, for I now know I come not only for the intellectual and sensory stimulation, I come for comfort. I come to be with humans I admire, with those who produced these drums and breathing dancers, who through the ages added beauty to this world. Their work gives me hope, reminds me that art is not a luxury: it nourishes our parched spirits. It is essential.

Do we all feel welcome in these usually hushed halls? "The majority take it as axiomatic that the museums are full of holy relics which refer to a mystery which excludes them: the mystery of unaccountable wealth," writes John Berger in *Ways of Seeing*.[1] I think again of how privileged I am to be in these quiet rooms, not having to wait for a free day—free in either sense, from job responsibilities or from admission fees. I am privileged to choose when I want to come. I can wander these galleries rather than, like many Latinas, having to care for someone else's children while mine are alone, or ironing clothes my employer will wear.

And certainly no-fee days and increased public programming—the democratization of museums—are an improvement from past eras, an acknowledgment that not only those defined as the washed and worthy deserve entrance. Museums are slowly changing, realizing that artifacts and art belong to all people, not some people. Recently Professor Teresa McKenna, a fellow museum lover and a member of the National Executive Committee of the exhibit "Chicano Art: Resistance and Affirmation, 1965–1985," shared with me her notion that a challenge of the exhibit was to bring public art into what has been deemed private space, elite space; to make private space, public. Anthropologist Alicia González, also a member of that committee, writes that one of the goals of this exhibit project, which should be the goal of all such projects, was to develop "a new model for the inclusion of underrepresented groups in the process of determining how to present those groups' cultural expressions to a diverse public."[2] Not exactly with alacrity, but some museums are becoming a bit embarrassed about how they acquired what they own, about why they arrogantly ushered certain groups past their polished doors. The faces viewing with me have become more varied in recent years. Not only audiences need to be diversified; museum staffs and the work exhibited need to reflect our national plurality, which will inevitably alter decisions about programming, priorities, presentation. Sally Price's *Primitive Art in Civilized Places* is a provocative reminder of assumptions that too often misguide museum presentation. She states that Westerners conveniently conclude that because " 'art' is an exclusively Western construct . . . Westerners [have] complete control over the aesthetic judgment of the world's art on the grounds that it would be culturally inappropriate to call on native aesthetic conceptualizations."[3] She further reminds us of a truth seldom admitted or discussed, yet applicable to all art forms, that "the 'eye' of even the most naturally gifted connoisseur is not naked, but views art through the lens of a Western cultural education."[4]

I walk on. I, who can barely sew a button, study an array of quilts, glad that such women's art is now displayed, think of the careful fingers—stitch, stitch, stitch—and probably careful voices that produced these works. The text of a bronze of Shiva says that her dance takes place within her heart. I study her and think of that dance, of the private nature of that spring of emotion. I watch a group of teenage girls walk by and wonder if they can hear or feel their private dance in a world that equates noise and brutality with entertainment.

The contemporary art halls most baffled my children when they were young. "Why, I could do that!" they would scoff, staring at a Jackson Pollock. I smile secretly when my youngest, now taller than I am, asks, "Where are our favorite rooms?"— meaning, yes, those rooms with massive canvases, with paint everywhere, the rooms that loosen me up inside, that provide escape from the confines of the predictable.

I walk outside, glad to breathe in sky and wind but also brimming with all I saw and felt, hearing the dance within my heart.

Notes

1. John Berger, *Ways of Seeing* (London: British Broadcasting Corporation, 1986), p. 24.

2. Alicia M. González and Edith Tonelli, "*Compañeros* and Partners: The CARA Project," in *Museums and Communities: The Politics of Public Culture*, Ivan Karp, Christine Mullen Kreamer, and Steven Levine (eds.) (Washington, D.C.: Smithsonian Institution Press, 1992), p. 266.

3. Sally Price, *Primitive Art in Civilized Places* (Chicago: University of Chicago Press, 1991), p. 89.

4. Price, *Primitive Art*, p. 93.

DESERT WOMEN

The desert.

How normal the starkness is when we live in it and know no other landscape. Geographical terrains are seldom awesome to their inhabitants. Many Mexican American women from the Southwest are desert women. We "know about survival / . . . Like cactus / we've learned to hoard."[1] We hoard what our mothers, our *tías,* our *abuelitas* hoarded: our values, our culture. Much as I want us, my daughters, my niece, Chicanas of all ages, to carry the positive aspects of our culture with them for sustenance, I also want us to question and ponder what values and customs we wish to incorporate into our lives, to continue our individual and our collective evolution. Such emergence, the wriggling from our past selves and experience as both women and women of Color, brings with it mixed blessings. We can learn from the desert, from the butterflies and snakes around us, how vulnerable a creature is in transition. We can offer one another strength and solace, protection from harsh elements, from the painful cold of sexism, racism, ageism, elitism; faith, the space for exploration.

Our cities are changing, though far too gradually. We have lived to see bicultural and bilingual librarians, principals, superintendents. We have lived to see Latinas as alderwomen, lawyers, doctors, judges, directors. Much as we want young people to view this as appropriate and normal, we want them to be keenly aware that Mexicans were part of this open, uncluttered Southwest landscape long before the arrival of Anglos. But women and men of Mexican descent have, like American Indians, been both excluded from shaping many aspects of their societies and unrecognized for the contributions they did make. Late in the last century, Anglos became the dominant culture. English, which had been foreign to our region, the language of the second colonizer, became the correct and valued language. Work viewed as menial too often became the province of the dark-skinned, of Mexicans. Ours.

Mexican women contributed to the intellectual history of this land of promise, the West, before the region was part of the United States. Thanks to the work of Chicana and Chicano literary historians such as Tey Diana Rebolledo, Rosaura Sánchez, and Clara Lomas, we are beginning to learn the names of some of the early women writers. How much all of us will profit from this research and from endeavors such as the ten-year Arte Público Press project funded by the Rockefeller Foundation, titled "Restoring the Hispanic Literary Heritage of the United States," which will publish work written from the colonial period to 1960.

"The struggles, lives and dreams of Hispanic women in the West from 1580 to 1940 is just beginning to be pieced together," Rebolledo tells us.[2] Women such as Nina Otero Warren, Cleofas Jaramillo, Fabiola Cabeza de Baca, Jovita González, and Josephina Niggli are finally receiving a degree of attention— women who sat in their long dresses, hearing the mix of indigenous languages, Spanish, and English that is part of our heritage, looking out at our mountains and moon, writing diaries, drama, fiction, poetry. For most of us, those women remain in the shadows. I think of them, pen poised above a sheet of blank paper, frowning, struggling as I do to find the right words.

But they were the exception. Most of our foremothers lived unsung lives, seldom if ever realizing their intellectual potential, renouncing personal ambition to give steadily and unstintingly to their families, to their children, to us. How they have worked—in their own homes and in the homes of others, in department stores, in churches, in fields, in canneries, in factories, in restaurants, in hospitals. Some supported their families financially, endured and endure; some supported husbands, endured and endure. We have drawn strength since we were in grade school from the pride of our female relatives. We were encouraged by the nods of approval from *Abuelita* when we recited the Pledge of Allegiance, even when she didn't understand a word we said, and perhaps even stubbornly refused to learn English, carving linguistic space for herself, denying those foreign sounds a place inside of her.

The prices have been high, then, for succeeding generations of Latinas to complete college and university educations. Often, "We are the first / of our people to walk this path."[3] The climate in our schools remains cold. Studies continue to reveal that educational institutions are not appropriately encouraging women of all ages and colors to explore their potential. Do we create a supportive climate for ourselves and for others? We know our students, female and male, need to study the history and literature of women. In a particular way, women of Color deserve role models to give them faith that they too can advance and contribute to society. As the educator James Banks reminds us, simply observing, for example, Hispanic Heritage Month and the quincentenary will not suffice. The educational system must be transformed. Our students should study Latina contributions, perspectives, and values as an integral part of their curriculum, a curriculum in which they see themselves. Textbooks that don't include diverse perspectives should be rejected by responsible educational institutions—for their bias *mis*-educates.

We, and all women, need and deserve our past. We can value the resourcefulness of our mothers and the homes they created, the space they shaped for us. There is much to be learned from the strengths of *tías* and *abuelitas,* and from our experiences in cooking, gardening, mothering. The seventeenth-century Mexican poet Sor Juana Inés de la Cruz quipped, "*Si Aristótoles hubiera guisado, mucho mas hubiera escrito.*" "Had Aristotle cooked, he would have written more."[4] Obviously, Sor Juana lived a privileged life and knew that housework can be true drudgery when a woman has no options. But rather than focusing on the drudgery of work, her words present such work as a source of creativity.

Our womanness, heritage, culture, language all deserve preservation. To transform our traditions wisely, we need to know them, learn from them, be inspired and saddened by them, choose for ourselves what to retain. But we can prize the past together, valuing the positive female and Mexican traditions. We can prize elements of the past as we persist in demanding, and creating, change. I remember looking up at a huge abandoned church outside of Ciudad Oaxaca and seeing a cactus somehow thriving and growing high up near the bell tower. I pointed to it in delight, and the Mexican with me said, "*Aun en los lugares mas dificiles el nopal da frutas.*" "Even in inhospitable places, cactus bears fruit."

Latinas are labeled a *double minority.* The words are depressing. They don't quite sound like "twice-blessed." Little wonder that most Latinas, whether in the Southwest or elsewhere in this country, don't dwell on this uncomfortable term. Anyway, who has time? We often are too busy playing the game of Great Expectations.

Most humans play some form of this game; most of us strive to fulfill the dreams that our society, our family, and our self have for us. Latinas, though, confront some unique challenges, and we often receive little support in fulfilling our potential.

In the eighties this country began to hear a Latin beat. Generations of determined women and men had questioned discriminatory hiring and promotion practices, immigration laws, inadequate heath-care systems, biased arts council panels, and had endured meeting after meeting requesting and ultimately demanding equal opportunities for our people. Singers, writers, and artists had worked to capture the vigor of *lo mejicano*. Their works are more and more visible. And demographics conspire with us. These population shifts, combined with historic equity struggles, mean we live in a society that finds it grudgingly necessary to notice our community. We can't ignore even this lukewarm willingness to respond to the needs of Latinos, whether by politicians, corporations, or federal or state agencies, because we know the grim statistics on wages and education for U.S. Latinos.

Ah, but our millions have billions to spend. Hundreds of millions are targeted by advertisers, who now like us and suddenly care deeply about our needs. Unlike those enmeshed in the political machinations of English Only, advertisers are happy to be bilingual. Well, their messages are. They speak to us *en español*. "*Ven es la hora de Miller*"; Coors tells us, "*Celebre! Cinco de mayo*"; Canadian Club says, "*¡Qué pareja! Canadian Club y tu!*" Xerox tells us that its Hispana employees are "*especial.*"

Advertisers track our values and thus our buying habits. Their analyses confirm the conclusions of psychologists and sociologists: we are loyal: to our families, the Spanish language, this country. Advertisers like loyalty, which they hope translates to brand-name loyalty. For those to whom English is a new language, brand names probably do bring a sense of security and predictability in the cacophony of strange noises. I remember that when my grandmother, who never spoke or wanted to speak English though all three of her children were born here, had a headache, only Bayer would do. She trusted the symbol on that small, pain-easing white circle.

Politicians, of course, are busy courting our loyalty too, because we are a young segment of an aging population. No more will candidates bite into a *tamal* with corn husk in place. Media visibility, the occasional Latina actor, the occasional Latino family in a commercial, can in an odd way foster a sense of group identity, even though cultural symbols are usually being appropriated, used. Our growing population makes it less threatening to delve into our cultural past, for what we discover suddenly interests people—perhaps because it is trendy, but the information nourishes us.

Such targeted marketing doesn't change the reality that this country often views us as either fiery, and thus less than rational, less than intellectual; or as docile, and thus less than effective, less than assertive. A woman named María might be considered as a candidate for a position as a domestic worker or secretary, but it is unlikely that she will seriously be considered as a candidate for senator. Yet. How easy is it, then, for a Latina to deal with a society that finds her dark eyes and hair attractive, but that is a bit surprised to see her aggressively pursuing a goal, striving to become an architect or veterinarian or literary critic? T'ain't easy.

And then there are our families. Intense emotional ties. Our parents, siblings, and relatives are a source of indescribable strength. Perhaps because marriage traditionally has been so important in our culture, men and our families often equate an attractive physical appearance with true womanhood. Many a *tía* or *abuelita* at home wants her niece to pursue a career, preferably in teaching or nursing, but *Tía* is secretly hoping— and probably praying—that we'll receive both a degree and a marriage proposal. She loves us and longs for some fine, respectful, hard-working man who will protect this vulnerable single woman from financial worries and the world's indifference.

Our parents also may do some frowning. How happy will they be at the news that we're considering joining the space program or applying for graduate school in another state? Frowns may really multiply once we're married with a family and announce that we need to begin traveling. Their frowns will say, "Neglect your children and husband? What kind of a woman are you?" Often their concern is genuine, and it is not easy to help them see that their desire to protect can be an unacknowledged desire to control.

Hard choices. We know women are socialized to please. How does a bright, talented Latina weather her family's displeasure when she works long hours rather than visiting regularly with sisters and cousins? *Tía*'s frowns have a way of giving us tired blood.

And what about the woman who gazes back in the mirror? What Great Expectations does she have for us? Chances are she wants us to look energetic, to excel in our chosen work, to struggle against injustice, to be a loving and respectful daughter, niece. Chances are she will never be quite satisfied with our efforts. She will be pressuring us, often relentlessly, to try harder, to produce better work. She can be our harshest critic. Convincing her to wink back at us occasionally may be a lifelong challenge.

The Latina who completes her college education—a small percentage of us—may indeed now have more opportunities, whether for employment or for service on panels, committees, and boards, which is appropriate. As double minorities committed to societal change, though, we find ourselves working doubly hard, struggling to prove to others that women like us are not a risk. We often feel tired, alone.

Alone, yet enmeshed in family responsibilities, concerned about our parents and siblings, about our children. And we worry about our national family or community as we hear the statistics about our growing Latina population. If Latinas have families—and fewer of us are marrying—they tend to be larger than the average, and more and more we head these families alone, often in poverty. Although we have high participation in the work force, we tend to be clerical or service workers. Our median income remains below that of Anglos. How well prepared are we for these challenges? How are we assisting other women to plan for the future, to have realistic expectations? Too many of us don't finish high school, too many of us who complete community college programs don't transfer to four-year institutions, too many of us are denied the opportunity to attend colleges away from home, too many of us are not encouraged fully to develop our talents.

As we mother, teach, write, mentor the next generation of women, we need to examine the lives of women in this country, our lives, not as we might want them to be, but as they are. It's difficult to change what we don't understand. What do we know about ourselves and about the women who will appear in our offices and classrooms? What do we know about our inside lives, the inside lives of the female middle class? Most women in the United States are not reading professional journals in their apartments or houses today. We ingest pollutants—toxic ideas and attitudes—while we watch movies and television or read steamy novels or relax with women's magazines. Women in this country continue to devour novels about women who find comfort in the image of being swept off tiny feet by determined, hard-muscled men.

We turn slick, musk-scented magazine pages that promise The Secrets of Skin Polish, 9 Ways to Prevent Wrinkles, Beauty from Head to Toe. For the price of the magazine, we are lured to believe that we can transform our flabby egos and disappointing bodies into the confident creatures who gaze boldly, sirens who beckon us to become perfect, smiling decorations. Listen to the bait. We are promised that we can be glamorous, attractive, radiant, exhilarating, classic, breathtaking, dazzling, legendary, mysterious. Similar magazines from Mexico promise that we can be *sensual, increíble, sexy, elegante, bella, enigmática*. We're taught the world over that it's our job to be pretty. Too often do we brood when we're five or eighty-five about our exteriors, peer in annoyance at our hips (too wide), noses (too long), lips (too thin). Some of us stop eating or eat until we're sick. We bare our unsatisfactory bodies so they can be reshaped, be made more lovable by surgeons who can mold us into beauty and happiness. How much time we spend looking the part, a part we didn't write.

In her documentary "A Famine Within," Katherine Gilday skillfully reveals our obsession with The Body, the difficulty we have accepting and loving ourselves, our imperfect selves. She shows how we are bombarded with images of women who seldom look like the women in our lives or in our mirror. Our shapes and the shapes of our mothers are steadily described as inferior, proof of our lack of self-control. We define others by their contours, equate thinness with morality. The young women Gilday interviews visibly struggle for words ugly enough to describe their reaction to being overweight. To be fat is to be "grotesque." Fashion models are often role models, says Gilday. Decorative, silent women.

Driving down the freeway, we see, "You've Come a Long Way, Baby." Baby? The woman smiling at us casually holding a cigarette is young, sleek, glamorous. Success is being defined for us as eternal youth, a carefree life, trendy clothes, and getting to do what men do—in this case, savor a health hazard. We want to define ourselves in broader and richer terms than that, but how do we help young women, all young women, to perceive such manipulation and to wrench their lives free from images that bind?

A *Time* cover story titled "Fighting the Backlash Against Feminism" (which should have been titled "Fighting the Backlash Against White Feminism"), includes a *Time*/CNN poll indicating that although the majority of respondents believe an active women's movement is still needed, the majority do not consider themselves feminists.[5] Our labels continue to separate us. And often the discussions are couched in militaristic terms: fighting, calls to arms, secret weapons, shock troops, guerrilla warfare, battle scarred. We need metaphors that inspire us to solve problems as communities, not armies. We need *una comunidad de conciencia,* "a community of conscience." We must liberate ourselves, but destruction and annihilation of those we oppose need not be the goal. Far harder, of course, to reach out our hands, our open, trusting hands, to others struggling to live their commitment to justice. Complex historical patterns of sexism, racism, ageism require our inventiveness and humanity even more than our anger, which in no way implies that just anger is invalid or inappropriate. But we must be determined to move through anger to creativity and power. Social psychologist Aída Hurtado and her colleagues who study issues of identity propose the term *social engagement* for a participatory process in which individuals "choose their own paths for themselves and their communities while still feeling a sense of contribution to a larger multicultural society."[6] We have a long way to go before we have educational institutions and a resulting society that nurture civic participation. At a deep level I wonder if the

United States really wants a nation of thinking citizens. Our support of education suggests not.

I took my children to see the remake of *Father of the Bride*, the only movie one Christmas that spared us bodies blown to blood before our eyes. I walked out annoyed at the end, surrounded by a satisfied, grinning crowd. It's a comforting, happy movie— if you're wealthy, white, or wanna-be. Oh, there is a Mexican in the film. The woman who smiles as she cleans the mansion. How many of us will sit in a dark theater munching popcorn, looking *up* at those beautiful homes with staircases to the sky, those laughing people in color-coordinated clothes, and be led, ever so gently to conclude that fathers who love their daughters write big checks? How many a young woman will return to her small home or apartment wishing, maybe even ashamed to be wishing, for such a cute life, a dad who plays basketball with her the night before she floats down the aisle in a dress light as clouds? How many of those wistful young women will be Native Americans, Asians, African Americans, Latinas?

We can appeal to young women's minds with our facts and statistics, but who is daily tugging at their hearts, at our hearts? Who keeps teaching heterosexual women to hum, "Some day my prince will come"? Most novels, magazines, movies, the "soaps" or *novelas,* the talk shows focus women's attention on the primacy of a snugly relationship with a man. Deep in their most private selves, do young women wait for their male solution, ashamed to admit this aloud, sparing themselves our cold frowns, the frowns of mothers, aunts, professors? They know what we want to hear, know all the right phrases and reasons— self-determination, self-interest, self-direction—but is their unspeakable truth that without *the* man at their side they just don't like themselves? We hand them Julia Álvarez's poem "Against

Cinderella." They read, "I can't believe it. / Whoever made it up is pulling my foot / so it'll fit that shoe." We say, Go on. They read the last words: "Some of us have learned to go barefoot / knowing the mate to one foot is the other."[7] Do they hear?

Even when they recognize the truth, can they make it part of themselves? We do not plan and prepare to be self-sustaining and autonomous; women are often underprepared to cope with daily stress by a society that steadily demands youth and beauty. If we want to communicate with women of all shapes and varieties, how do we create spaces not only for our private selves but also for our collective selves? Spaces where we can together admit our dreams and fears, using our emotions as resources for discovery?

The truth is that womanhood is defined for us so effectively by advertisers that we're being naïve if we think we can escape. How do those of us who care about women—about our daughters, nieces, students, friends—assist them more accurately to assess the realities they will confront? More than half of the women in this country work outside the home. More than half of those women are single, widowed, separated, or divorced. Dollar per dollar, we still earn less than men. Most of the child-rearing responsibilities remain ours. We can tell young women to plan, prepare, preserve, persist; but I doubt that they hear us, because in their minds they are walking into the sun, into a boy's (or man's) smile. Even naming ourselves is difficult. Feminist scholar Carolyn Heilbrun reminds us that "women have long been nameless. They have not been persons. Handed by a father to another man, the husband, they have been objects of circulation, exchanging one name for another."[8]

Some men are attempting to ease the pressures felt by their working mothers, sisters, wives. The change is slow and difficult. Our children see our exhaustion. We have two-career families but not enough two-parent families even in two-parent homes. My daughters may have even a more difficult time than I did because their expectations of what they can and should achieve both personally and professionally are higher.

I think of them, both so bright and full of life, studying hard to complete their university educations, and I worry. Given the constant bombardment by the media, the images of slender female bodies, tight clothes, alluring makeup, men's muscular bodies, soft romance, hard sex; the layering of images, smiling women with men, lonely women without, children, happy children with their mothers, at home, the houses, cars, never new enough. How do I prepare them for life's deceptions and inequities, for this society's patterns of shaping gender to guarantee consumption? How can my small voice be heard above the throbbing din? How do I nudge them to dream, as does the protagonist in Sandra Cisneros's short story "Bien Pretty," of "real women. The ones I've known everywhere except on TV, in books and magazines . . . Passionate *and* powerful, tender and volatile, brave. And, above all, fierce."[9]

We can encourage women not to be deceived by the glamour-girl illusion, remind them to consider not what they'll wear when they drive off into the sunset but how they'll develop the internal strength needed to nurture their talents. We can consciously and conscientiously indicate to women of all ages, whether in our classes or in our conversations, that we are interested in their search for self-worth. We can struggle to resist basing our expectations of women, including ourselves, on ethnicity, age, class, sexual preference, physical disabilities. We can resist demeaning women's traditional work and women who choose traditional roles. *Siendo muy mujer,* being a real woman in the traditional sense, need no longer mean only fingers adept at cooking and crocheting. It can mean contributing to society in a unique way. Such redefinition and freedom requires internal and external struggle, but being stifled, repressing one's voice and talents is unhealthy, and ultimately more painful.

Persistence is essential. I often joke that if my résumé listed my rejections instead of my publications, it would be much, much longer. I read a wonderful poem and essay by Donald Hall the other day. It ended by saying that the poem took two or three years to write and more than a hundred drafts. Students usually consider one draft sufficient.

Latinas face significant challenges, given the stereotypes embedded in the national psyche and the sexism of our culture, a culture that often rewards us for being pretty, long-suffering, and selfless. We need to listen to one another and to draw strength from one another. I remember hearing professor Margarita Melville talk to a group of university students, watching her teach them about the importance of group identity for self-assurance, of seeking mentors, of cultivating a sense of belonging. That last bit of wisdom, of saying to myself, "I have the right to be here," has helped me innumerable times.

Many of us have endured personal stings, the pain of being the lone voice, the token, the thorn in the side of our offices and institutions, seeking justice for our culture in these United States. Often we receive "bitter frowns / in committees and board rooms / push and pound, push and pound / "Why am I the only Mexican American here?" [10] At times we grow angry at a city, a state, a country that we love but that often ignores us. On difficult days we are "Legal Aliens" in our own land,

> viewed by Anglos as perhaps exotic,
> perhaps inferior, definitely different,
> viewed by Mexicans as alien
> (their eyes say, "You may speak
> Spanish but you're not like me").[11]

Just as each of us is the product of two very different parents, those of us who are Mexican Americans are the products of two very different cultures. Mexico is the warmer parent, but we live, and many of us were born, in the United States and rightfully should be heard. We love this cold house. It is home. But we were taught to value people, the importance of the heart.

Writers such as Margarita Cota-Cárdenas urge us to look for our true names inside of ourselves: *"Busca tu nombre / dentro de ti misma."* [12] Even extricating ourselves long enough from the mesh of family and work to be able to examine the pressures of being a Mexican American woman requires significant effort and determination.

How do we create space for ourselves to be ourselves, our multiple Latina, Hispana, Mexicana, Chicana selves? Space in ourselves to hear ourselves, space free of the pollution of bigotry and bias, space free of contemporary colonizers. Space for play and dance. Some day I want to write about preserving the imp in ourselves, the light side, like the little girl I saw one night at an ice-cream shop who was dancing by herself, only vaguely aware that a group was watching her, dancing for herself. The desert teaches us the value of space. Like the wind, our spirits will play if set free in a broad expanse. The inventiveness and creativity that shrivel in the tiny box labeled Only a Chicana burst like the fireworks that signal independence in July.

Desert Women

Desert women know
about survival.
Fierce heat and cold
have burned and thickened
our skin. Like cactus
we've learned to hoard,

to sprout deep roots,
to seem asleep, yet wake
at the scent of softness
in the air, to hide
pain and loss by silence,
no branches wail
or whisper our sad songs
safe behind our thorns.

Don't be deceived.
When we bloom, we stun.[13]

Each generation seeks to evolve. In new circumstances Latinas and other women today are wrestling with the old human riddle, How do I live in the present to change the future? With sociologist Patricia Hill Collins, we know that "subordinate groups have long had to use alternative ways to create independent self-definitions and self-valuations and to rearticulate them through our own specialists."[14] We want to change because we know that our schools don't appropriately include the legacies of past generations of women. We are aware that women's voices, and certainly Latina voices, are not being sufficiently heard in the arts, sciences, education, health, social services, and government; that poverty is more and more a women's issue; that we want fairer options for our daughters.

It is leaders, Latinas willing to take risks, to speak out, to band together, who will also be an unstoppable force; insisting on equity for ourselves and our daughters, remembering that we are the lucky ones who have received the gift of an education. *Se hace camino al andar.* (In walking, we make a road.) We will be making many roads at times, physically alone but strengthened by the knowledge that we are together, refusing to subject one another, in Anzaldúa's words, to "ethnic legitimacy tests."[15]

We must remember women struggling for literacy, safe homes, adequate health care, accessible services, a fair wage, diplomas and degrees, personal choice. They are with us, preventing us from becoming too comfortable in our protected offices and lives. What literary critic Sonia Saldívar-Hull writes about the title story from Sandra Cisneros's widely acclaimed collection *Woman of Hollering Creek* is the hope of Chicana writers: "Cisneros shows how feminist solidarity, the *feminismo popular* that many Chicanas and *mexicanas* in Greater Mexico engage, puts theory into practice and begins to cross the border geopolitically and across class lines."[16]

And there is happiness in this struggle, happiness that counters the wounds. Together we become less timid, more confident that we are not subversives or disloyal when we seek justice. There is an appropriateness to our insistence on equity from our stubborn cities, states, country.

Women working to produce necessary change and thus leading fragmented lives see ourselves discussed and analyzed. Pop psychologists offer us Oil of Olé for our psyches, quick cures for what some term our persistent insecurity. I choose not to reduce our motivations entirely to a drive to prove our personal worth. Many women, though tired, rushed, guilty, underpaid, and undervalued, are trying to create space for the next generation of women. When we're thinking clearly, we are transforming our homes and workplaces, rather than, as traditionally done, transforming ourselves to suit our circumstances.

As we prize the past together, valuing the positive traditions, we can also participate together in changing the present, in creating new traditions. Much as I want a community or communities of women working together, I want individual women to allow for private time, to be fully present in the present, to preserve our ability to care, to support one another, to take risks, to be candid yet sensitive with one another. She who laughs, lasts. We need time for renewal, lest work lull us into drones. Let's nudge one another to nurture our best selves by allowing space for play in our lives, be that time to read, think, dream, hike, garden, travel, dance, to be creative with our selves.

Women. We gather—in our homes, neighborhoods, committees, conferences, communities. More and more we gather internationally at conferences such as "New Visions of Leadership: 1992 Global Forum of Women," held in Dublin in 1992. We gather to explore our shared values: concern for the young and for the environment, for justice, which precedes peace. Let's accept the power of being the majority in this world; let's create an international community of women of conscience, multilingual, multivocal, multicolored, united by beliefs such as that expressed in the Balinese prayer, "May all that breathes be well." Truly, well. And until that day, we are united by our *inquietudes,* our unrest at injustice, our determination to have every creature safe and valued. Rather than defining power as domination or control, we can define womanpower—*el poder de la mujer*—as energy, as collaboration. Ours can be an alternative vision. The perspective that values not dominance but respect for all life, the well-being of individuals of all colors, sizes, and ages, that can love and lead, has critical lessons for this world.

Those of us who went to school in this country year after year memorized words written by Emma Lazarus, although as a child I never heard the name of the woman who wrote the words on the Statue of Liberty, nor do I remember ever hearing the beginning of her sonnet:

Not like the brazen giant of Greek fame,
With conquering limbs astride from land to land;
Here at our sea-washed, sunset gates shall stand
A mighty woman with a torch, whose flame

Is the imprisoned lightning, and her name
Mother of Exiles.

Perhaps our most significant challenge is how we Latinas resist contemporary colonization. Indeed, we can resist believing
the demeaning myths about us both as women and Mexicans.
Theorist Chela Sandoval writes about the skill we daily use to
resist patterns or traditions that limit us, a skill she describes as
a "differential mode of oppositional consciousness."[17] We know
how to alter our language or style, how to position ourselves,
to oppose those around us, whether our mothers, colleagues,
employers or institutions, when their behavior or comments de-
mean us or our community. Knowing how to determine the
most effective form of resistance, says Sandoval, requires "grace,
flexibility, and strength."[18] Through history, experience, and necessity, we know how best to push against those persons or ideas
that will smother us. United, we free ourselves of having to invest all of our individual strength in resistance. United, we can
invite ourselves to create. United we withstand the steady disap-
pointments and rejection, and we individually and collectively
raise our voices, more and more tell and write and sing and
paint our own stories, create our own grand buildings, bridges,
theories and myths, refusing to be limited by the expectations
of others. By incorporating the strength and stubbornness of
nuestras antepasadas, "our foremothers," we create and claim *our*
space, the space to be our surprising selves.

Notes

1. Pat Mora, "Desert Women," in *Borders* (Houston: Arte Público Press,
1986), p. 80.
2. Tey Diana Rebolledo, "Introduction," in *Infinite Divisions: An Anthology of Chicano Literature*, edited by Tey Diana Rebolledo and Eliana
Rivero (Tucson: University of Arizona Press, forthcoming, 1993).

3. Pat Mora, "University Avenue," in *Borders*, p. 19.

4. Margaret Sayers Peden, *A Woman of Genius: The Intellectual Autobiography of Sor Juana Inés de la Cruz* (Salisbury, Conn.: Lime Rock Press, 1987), p. 62.

5. Nancy Gibbs, "The War Against Feminism," *Time*, 9 March 1992, p. 54.

6. Aída Hurtado, "Latinos and Anglos in the United States: Interdependent Collective Representations" (Paper presented at the Conference on Social Structure, Culture, and Cognition, University of Michigan, Ann Arbor, June 1991), p. 10.

7. Julia Álvarez, "Against Cinderella," in *Florilegia* (Corvallis, Oreg.: Calyx Books, 1987), p. 174.

8. Carolyn G. Heilbrun, *Writing a Woman's Life* (New York: Ballantine Books, 1988), p. 121.

9. Sandra Cisneros, "Bien Pretty," in *Woman of Hollering Creek* (New York: Random House, 1991), p. 161.

10. Pat Mora, "Withdrawal Symptoms," in *Borders*, p. 26.

11. Pat Mora, "Legal Alien," in *Chants* (Houston: Arte Público Press, 1984), p. 52.

12. Margarita Cota-Cárdenas, *"Justo Será,"* in *Noches despertando en consciencias* (Tucson, Ariz.: Scorpion Press, 1975), n.p.

13. Mora, "Desert Women," in *Borders*, p. 80.

14. Patricia Hill Collins, *Black Feminist Thought* (New York: Routledge, 1990), p. 202.

15. Gloria Anzaldúa, *"En Rapport,* In Opposition: *Cobrando cuentas a las nuestras,"* in *Making Face, Making Soul: Haciendo Caras*, ed. Gloria Anzaldúa (San Francisco: Aunt Lute Foundation, 1990), p. 143.

16. Sonia Saldívar-Hull, " *'Ya Soy Mujer'*: Crossing the Border/Changing the Subject in Chicana/Mexicana Discourse," in *Rearticulations: The Practice of Chicano Cultural Studies*, ed. Mario García (Los Angeles and Berkeley: University of California Press, forthcoming).

17. Chela Sandoval, *U.S. Third World Feminism: The Theory and Method of Oppositional Consciousness in the Postmodern World*, Genders, no. 10, (Austin: University of Texas Press, 1991), p. 15.

18. Sandoval, *U.S. Third World Feminism*, p. 15.

7

REMEMBERING LOBO

We called her *Lobo*. The word means "wolf" in Spanish, an odd name for a generous and loving aunt. Like all names it became synonymous with her, and to this day returns me to my childself. Although the name seemed perfectly natural to us and to our friends, it did cause frowns from strangers throughout the years. I particularly remember one hot afternoon when on a crowded streetcar between the border cities of El Paso and Juárez, I momentarily lost sight of her. "Lobo! Lobo!" I cried in panic. Annoyed faces peered at me, disappointed at such disrespect to a white-haired woman.

Actually the fault was hers. She lived with us for years, and when she arrived home from work in the evening, she'd knock on our front door and ask, "*¿Dónde estan mis lobitos?*" "Where are my little wolves?"

Gradually she became our lobo, a spinster aunt who gathered the four of us around her, tying us to her for life by giving us all she had. Sometimes to tease her we would call her by her real name. "*¿Dónde esta Ignacia?*" we would ask. Lobo would laugh and say, "She is a ghost."

To all of us in nuclear families today, the notion of an extended family under one roof seems archaic, complicated. We treasure our private space. I will always marvel at the generosity of my parents, who opened their door to both my grandmother and Lobo. No doubt I am drawn to the elderly because I grew up with two entirely different white-haired women who worried about me, tucked me in at night, made me tomato soup or hot *hierbabuena* (mint tea) when I was ill.

Lobo grew up in Mexico, the daughter of a circuit judge, my grandfather. She was a wonderful storyteller and over and over told us about the night her father, a widower, brought his grown daughters on a flatbed truck across the Rio Grande at the time of the Mexican Revolution. All their possessions were left in Mexico. Lobo had not been wealthy, but she had probably never expected to have to find a job and learn English.

When she lived with us, she worked in the linens section of a local department store. Her area was called "piece goods and bedding." Lobo never sewed, but she would talk about materials she sold, using words I never completely understood, such as *pique* and *broadcloth*. Sometimes I still whisper such words just to remind myself of her. I'll always savor the way she would order "sweet milk" at restaurants. The precision of a speaker new to the language.

Lobo saved her money to take us out to dinner and a movie, to take us to Los Angeles in the summer, to buy us shiny black shoes for Christmas. Though she never married and never bore children, Lobo taught me much about one of our greatest challenges as human beings: loving well. I don't think she ever discussed the subject with me, but through the years she lived her love, and I was privileged to watch.

She died at ninety-four. She was no sweet, docile Mexican woman dying with perfect resignation. Some of her last words before drifting into semiconsciousness were loud words of annoyance at the incompetence of nurses and doctors.

"No sirven." "They're worthless," she'd say to me in Spanish.

"They don't know what they're doing. My throat is hurting and they're taking X-rays. Tell them to take care of my throat first."

I was busy striving for my cherished middle-class politeness. "Shh, shh," I'd say. "They're doing the best they can."

"Well, it's not good enough," she'd say, sitting up in anger.

Lobo was a woman of fierce feelings, of strong opinions. She was a woman who literally whistled while she worked. The best way to cheer her when she'd visit my young children was to ask for her help. Ask her to make a bed, fold laundry, set the table or dry dishes, and the whistling would begin as she moved about her task. Like all of us, she loved being needed. Understandable, then, that she muttered in annoyance when her body began to fail her. She was a woman who found self-definition and joy in visibly showing her family her love for us by bringing us hot *té de canela* (cinnamon tea) in the middle of the night to ease a cough, by bringing us comics and candy whenever she returned home. A life of giving.

One of my last memories of her is a visit I made to her on November 2, *El Día de los Muertos,* or All Souls' Day. She was sitting in her rocking chair, smiling wistfully. The source of the smile may seem a bit bizarre to a U.S. audience. She was fondly remembering past visits to the local cemetery on this religious feast day.

"What a silly old woman I have become," she said. "Here I sit in my rocking chair all day on All Souls' Day, sitting when I should be out there. At the cemetery. Taking good care of *mis muertos,* my dead ones.

"What a time I used to have. I'd wake while it was still dark outside. I'd hear the first morning birds, and my fingers would almost itch to begin. By six I'd be having a hot bath, dressing carefully in black, wanting *mis muertos* to be proud of me, proud to have me looking respectable and proud to have their graves taken care of. I'd have my black coffee and plenty of toast.

You know the way I like it. Well browned and well buttered. I wanted to be ready to work hard.

"The bus ride to the other side of town was a long one, but I'd say a rosary and plan my day. I'd hope that my perfume wasn't too strong and yet would remind others that I was a lady.

"The air at the cemetery gates was full of chrysanthemums: that strong, sharp, fall smell. I'd buy tin cans full of the gold and wine flowers. How I liked seeing aunts and uncles who were also there to care for the graves of their loved ones. We'd hug. Happy together.

"Then it was time to begin. The smell of chrysanthemums was like a whiff of pure energy. I'd pull the heavy hose and wash the gravestones over and over, listening to the water pelting away the desert sand. I always brought newspaper. I'd kneel on the few patches of grass, and I'd scrub and scrub, shining the gray stones, leaning back on my knees to rest for a bit and then scrubbing again. Finally a relative from nearby would say, '*Ya, ya, Nacha,*' and laugh. Enough. I'd stop, blink my eyes to return from my trance. Slightly dazed, I'd stand slowly, place a can of chrysanthemums before each grave.

"Sometimes I would just stand there in the desert sun and listen. I'd hear the quiet crying of people visiting new graves; I'd hear families exchanging gossip while they worked.

"One time I heard my aunt scolding her dead husband. She'd sweep his gravestone and say, '*¿Porqué?* Why did you do this, you thoughtless man? Why did you go and leave me like this? You know I don't like to be alone. Why did you stop living?' Such a sight to see my aunt with her proper black hat and her fine dress and her carefully polished shoes muttering away for all to hear.

"To stifle my laughter, I had to cover my mouth with my hands."

• • •

I see Lobo in that afternoon sun, and I wonder if the sharp smell of chrysanthemums on her fingertips startled her. Surely she wanted to save it, to save the day, to horde the pleasure of using the love trapped inside all year long. I imagine how she must have enjoyed the feeling of strength in her arms as she scrubbed those graves, loving the notion that her relatives' markers would be the cleanest in the cemetery. They would sparkle.

Bizarre? Bizarre to find happiness in a cemetery? Perhaps, but understanding that attitude toward death—and love—is a key to understanding the growing U.S. Latino population. Family ties are so strong that not even death can sever them. Although Emily Dickinson writes of "sweeping up the Heart / and putting love away / We shall not want to use again / Until Eternity," Mexicans don't always do this. Such tidiness eludes us.

Explanations for such attitudes abound: Indian beliefs of life and death as a continuum, the strong influence of the Catholic Church with its tenets about the soul and afterlife. Somehow we continue to want to openly demonstrate our love. Lobo's annual cemetery excursions were, yes, a testimony to family pride, but also a testimony to her enduring love for family members.

I wonder if, as she sat before me that last November 2, her arms ached as love pushed against the inside of her skin, trying to find a way out. Her emotional pain at her trapped love, at no longer being able to use her body to help her loved ones—living and dead—was probably as distressing as the physical pain of arthritis. Such capacity for love is as startling as the scent of chrysanthemums.

I have no desire to put my love for Lobo away. Quite the contrary, I don't want to forget: I want to remember. My tribute to her won't be in annual pilgrimages to a cemetery. I was born in these United States and am very much influenced by this culture. But I do want to polish, polish my writing tools to preserve images of women like Lobo, unsung women whose fierce family love deserves our respect. Lobo has been dead almost ten years now. I will always miss her physical presence in my life, her laughter. She's not one to stay out of my life, though. She manages to slip into every book of poetry I write. Her poem for poetry book four is already written, and my first children's book is about her ninetieth birthday party. She danced.

Bailando

I will remember you dancing,
spinning round and round
a young girl in Mexico,
your long, black hair free in the wind,
spinning round and round
a young woman at village dances
your long, blue dress swaying
to the beat of *La Varsoviana*
smiling into the eyes of your parents,
years later smiling into my eyes
when I'd reach up to dance with you
my dear aunt, who years later
danced with my children,
you, white-haired but still young
waltzing on your ninetieth birthday,
more beautiful than the orchid
pinned on your shoulder,
tottering now when you walk
but saying to me, "*Estoy bailando,*"
and laughing.[1]

Notes

1. Pat Mora, "Bailando," in *Chants* (Houston: Arte Público Press, 1984), p. 51.

MY FIERCE MOTHER

My mother is cleaning closets. This may hardly seem a remarkable occurrence. In fact, this activity is considered normal, motherly. I once worked with a woman who so relished the pleasure of throwing away the clothes, magazines, and papers accumulated throughout a year that she would spend her vacations sorting and dusting in her trailer and return to the office psychologically cleansed.

Not my mom. Not that our house was ever messy. Quite the contrary. She tells me that when she was first married and lived in what became home to her four children, she would clean all day. In the late afternoon, she would sit and study the straightness of picture frames and curtains. But she was a hoarder. I can remember summer days when I'd decide to bring order to the unseen—medicine cabinets, drawers, closets. My mother would laugh, saying, "You know I'm a pack rat, Dear."

Given how intelligent my mother is, I've always regretted that she wasn't given the opportunity that she and my father gave each of us: the opportunity to attend college. She was an outstanding high school student, but she graduated during the Depression. Even the little money she made at a downtown department store was needed, particularly as she was the eldest in her family. Neither of her parents spoke English.

My maternal grandparents met and married in this country, which would house them until they died yet maybe never be their home. My grandfather, who died before my parents married, never permitted English spoken in his presence. "*Cuando entras a esta casa, hija, pisas México.*" "When you enter this house, Daughter, you are in Mexico." My mother and her brothers were bilingual. She has always said that her mother would grumble that her daughter learned English to be able to fight with the neighbors. My mother always loved public speaking; she competed at the state level in speech contests. She still wonders how she did this. The spunk necessary may be related to the present closet cleaning. After almost twenty years in their apartment and more than fifty years of marriage accumulating pictures and papers, my mother is sorting. With enthusiasm she's sorting through her life.

Of late she has been particularly cheery on the phone. She tells me the dining room table is covered with piles. She's separating each of our stacks of certificates and diplomas. She's pondering which of her possessions to leave to each child and grandchild. I can imagine all the different versions my father is hearing as he tries unsuccessfully to watch a boxing match on television in quiet. I sense a secret delight in her process, in thinking of ways to reveal to those she loves that she does really know who and what we are. That she really *has* been listening all these years.

My children frown when I mention her present flurry of activity. It seems a distasteful admission of death. How decidedly inconvenient of her, so close to her birthday, to yield what she's saved, to scrutinize the contents of her shelves and cabinets with a critical eye. What do I give a person who is dividing her wealth? I'm struck by the irony.

Now my mother would find humor in my use of the word *wealth* here. It is not only the young whose definitions are influenced by the consumerism we breathe, our habit of equating wealth with money. And indeed it would be more accurate to say that she's dividing the symbols, for her wealth has been steadily given to us year after year.

It is difficult to know how to convey that to a mother, how to say that I was listening to her too, that I know who and what she is because she shared not just her body where I roomed comfortably for nine months, but her essence, her spirit. She has made decisions about her energy, time, and money because they would be good for me and my siblings. She is *Mom* in the emotionally laden sense of that word.

Even before she saw me, she began to care for me, to eat right so that I would begin life in good health. She nursed me so that I would have more immunities. She taught me English and Spanish so that I could derive pleasure from two cultures. She stayed up with me at night when I was sick and saw to it that I learned to swim, even though water terrified her. She was always there: at PTA meetings, school parties, piano recitals, graduations.

And she read every paper I wrote and took to her, helping me rephrase those awkward words. She was there to help me care for each of my babies, and though my children are grown, she still worries about me if I'm on a trip or alone. She saves every piece I write and any piece written about me, which returns us to her hoarding.

Somehow stating what she did does not convey what she is. Maybe those years of high school speech contests helped prepare her to demand her rights. I've never seen anyone intimidate my mother, who is about five feet tall. Without cheating and resorting to physical violence, I can't imagine anyone who could—not a president, prime minister, or pope. I smile, aware that her doctors know what happens if she is kept waiting. She storms out. Storms at seventy-four. A firm letter or phone call will soon follow.

When she's angry, I think her eyes can melt metal. She is assertively articulate in English or Spanish and has never hesitated to state her displeasure, whether at poor service, rude behavior, or injustice. She can be bilingually fierce.

Articulate fire is wealth, and while she was hoarding pictures and mementos, she was sharing that wealth. When we transgressed, we felt the sting of her words. Ultimately, of course, she was showing us the importance of expecting justice and of clearly and forcefully stating objections to unfairness.

My youngest, Cecilia, is also cleaning her closet this month, though not by choice. That "curl of light . . . who rocked inside me"[1] is beginning to sort through what will go with her to college and what can be discarded. Like my mother, she has always been a saver. As a child, she would cry when I would walk into her room, brown bags in hand, ready to sit with her while she reluctantly cleaned drawers, admitted that not every scrap of paper crammed into the shelves at the bottom of her closet merited keeping. Once I discovered pull-off tabs from Kleenex boxes carefully hidden under a doll mattress. It was her newest collection. This is the child who also saved the paper circles from hole punchers. Her confetti, she called it. Perhaps she so valued every scrap she touched that she just couldn't bear to discard it, and shoved her drawings and yarn scraps into every corner and crevice of her closet, hoping I wouldn't notice. Her accumulated possibilities that might prove useful in the future.

So two women I love are cleaning closets. The younger has "honey / hair, freckles, eyes aglow."[2] Spun gold, I tease her. Cissy inherited all that gold from Amelia—Mamande to me— her sweet maternal great-grandmother. My hope is that she will inherit much more from her grandmother, Estella, than the objects being so lovingly set aside for her. What I wish for her is her grandmother's articulate fierceness, her determination to be treated fairly.

Notes

1. Pat Mora, "*Mañanitas:* Birthday Song," in *Borders* (Houston: Arte Público Press, 1986), p. 38.
2. Mora, "*Mañanitas:* Birthday Song," p. 38.

A CONVERSATION
WITH MY THREE

I know, just like me to call it a conversation when I get to do all the talking. Almost twenty-five years of parenting have taught me that sometimes to be heard, I have to resort to devious means.

Next month we will all be together for the last high school graduation in our family, and as we've learned in previous springs, graduations bring advice much as rain brings new sprouts. Everywhere. Family, friends, and even strangers will be saying to anyone under thirty, "Work hard, save money." Even people who don't know our graduate will smile when she rushes by, hands pressing her square cap in place on her red hair, grin wide as the robe ballooning behind her.

Teachers will congratulate the graduates, speakers who have prepared carefully will share what they've learned, trying to inspire the distracted to shape a meaningful life. Eloquently and appropriately, they will exhort the faces before them, each glowing like a full moon, to care for their physical being, to care for this earth, to use their talents and energy to improve this complex world, to be resourceful self-learners, to be inquisitive, to know their past and to shape their future. We will hear about justice, moral courage, passion, and compassion. We will be challenged to think about risk and vision and values.

As a mother, I find graduations a test of my emotional will. Even when one of you isn't graduating, once I hear "Pomp and Circumstance," I think of you, moving in long robes, the bodies I knew so well and now don't know at all, my altered flesh moving in measured steps while I dig my nails into my palms. Partially I blame the music. Marches change my body chemistry. My bones dissolve. Emotions trapped inside my body press against my skin. So do words. I struggle to joke the ache away.

I think of the private shiver you each feel when you pull on the graduation gown, when you look at yourself in the mirror. Pride, sadness, disbelief, apprehension. Because a significant portion of the population still does not graduate from high school, successfully completing the courses, surviving the quizzes, research papers, and finals remains cause for applause. And although you've each been wildly anxious to flee the burdensome building where you spent four long years, waiting for that last moment when you could scream the call of the free as you run for a last time through those halls, you know that the predictable days and faces safely ordered your days—and nights. You know that friends who can now finish your sentences will soon scrutinize you with curiosity.

Even though you studied year after year, resenting assurances that you would indeed graduate one day, you are still a bit surprised to see your familiar face above the serious garment. It feels like Halloween. The robes will be tossed aside, but we all know: you are changing your life.

Because I have so much to say on such occasions, I may say little about what I'm feeling. I hug you, hand you a present, a slice of cake. Later send a card or letter in which I try to say what's in my heart. Perhaps I write and urge you to follow the advice of my friend Blas Santos, a wise man from the Dominican Republic, who aims for balance in his life by allocating time for family and friends, time for work, time for those less fortunate, time for self. Perhaps I try to warn you about life's dangers. Beware of money. It can convince you that you are better than the waitress who takes your order. You are not. Beware of cynics. Their stale breaths can shrivel your fragile hopes.

You are changing your life, your exterior life. And I want to seize the occasion, seize the scents and sights of spring with all the whispered possibilities, saying: look to your interior.

I remember when each of you first shaped your breath into a word. I worked to lure your inside out. I tempted you with the world outside yourself, where your body would live, saying, look, feel, taste, smell, listen; sun, thorn, mango, perfume, song. I wanted to entrance you. The spell, I fear, is hard to break. Our own exterior, whether bare or dressed in cap or gown, and the jangling world around us want our constant attention. We decorate: our bodies, our homes, our offices, our cities. The mirrors and glitter hypnotize. *Mira. Mira. Mira.* Look. Look. Look. Life on the outside.

Look to your interior.

You say you look but can't see anything; how can you look at what's not there? I say look *to,* as in care for, as in heed. We are fragile through and through. What we ignore can vanish, like mist. The interior life has always been endangered.

Listen. In Guatemala, the quetzal lives in cloud forests. With its beak, it carefully picks *aguacatillo,* a hard, green fruit about the size of a cherry. Its breast feathers burn red, the blood of conquered Maya, legend says. Its tail feathers gleam iridescent green and blue. They are longer than your arm. Now watch. When the quetzal dives straight down the cold mountain, its plumes rise and fall, green waves on the willing wind, an ocean of feathers. *Tak-teek, tak-teek,* the bird cries. Did you hear it? Did you hear the feathers rising and falling like old music? Follow. Let it fly inside you for a bit. The space is wide. Its feathers move your air. If caged, the quetzal dies.

In you dwells a spirit even more rare; in fact, unique. Only you will ever hear its every sound, though you must listen. Wanting to know this spirit is wanting to know who you are and who you are becoming, what you think and feel, all you can imagine. To know requires silence. Take long walks on quiet paths far from cities. Lose yourself, your skin and bones, listen so intently to a pond or poem or painting that you fall in, fall in to your interior life. This is not dreaming; this is moving through nature and art to reach your self. And then listen, surprised at what you hear. Sometimes it is an imp you release and follow, a sprite who dances anywhere. Sometimes it is a figure of endless patience who takes you deeper and deeper into the light.

As a family we will gather through the years to witness a life-change symbolized by ceremony, special music, and garments and words. These are important events. We humans are social creatures; we communicate through ceremony. But we are also private beings, and perhaps our most significant changes are internal, what we call mind, heart, soul, spirit. It is in a carefully cultivated interior world that we discover our possibilities for a more noble life. Don't abandon your Self.

"*Dime con quien andas y te diré quien eres.*" "Tell me with whom you walk, and I will tell you who you are." Listen. If all you hear is talk of career mobility, exercise, military prowess, vacations—flee. Cultivating a life that is more than acquisition and activity, that allows time and space for thought and imagination, for resisting the distractions, metaphors, issues, and solutions that others impose, requires strength; the strength to save yourself, to push the world away enough so that you can see it. Measure your life by what you give.

My wishes for you are many: health, joy, travel, friends, laughter, family, a sense of mission. I've always hoped that the world would be better because you three are here. I am. Think of the quetzal, how it entrusts its life to the invisible, swoops into the unknown as we must swoop into ourselves if we are truly to change our lives.

10

SNAPSHOTS
Puerto Vallarta

Click.

Another snapshot. Another U.S. tourist preserving on film the lushness of Puerto Vallarta. I too some years ago participated in the ritual; posed my children on the beach, in the pool, by the hibiscus. And I could have taken countless more pictures than my conservative judgement allowed: the sun slipping from behind a gold cloud silently into the water, the frigate birds gliding like huge black kites above the sunbathers, the surprise of pink, fuchsia, red, and gold bougainvillea—all blooming on one wrought-iron fence. To a desert denizen, the overabundance of Puerto Vallarta was startling. The senses almost reel at waves of water to the horizon, hills of palm trees, platters of fresh lobster, shrimp, red snapper; bowls of pineapple, papayas, cantaloupe.

Click. Click.

Like most rituals, picture taking has value. We are preserving memories, recording our journey on this earth. Rituals also have rules. Unless we are particularly boorish, there are snapshots we don't take. Often these images are the more revealing glimpses of another place. They are the disturbing realities rather than the comforting postcard scenes.

90

What realities should linger long after our tans have disappeared?

I want to remember the soldiers with tommy guns sauntering in twos along the beach. Dark uniforms, dark laughter. I was told they were patrolling because it was peak tourist season in Mexico. "Last year many cameras were stolen on this beach," said the soft-spoken waiter. "That's why the soldiers are here." And the soldiers seemed to be enjoying the assignment, walking in the sand among the greased bodies. Laughing. I kept wondering, Would you shoot? Would you really shoot?

I want to remember the mother and daughter who sold T-shirts on the beach. Each morning they would weave their way, saying, "*Playeras. Playeras.*" All colors, all sizes. Tourists enjoyed dickering, enjoyed having wares brought to them, enjoyed removing thousand-peso bills from their wallets and receiving a handful of change. The little girl would run to bring her mother a requested size, color, style. But the little girl wore a plain white T-shirt with numerous holes. Like so many in Mexico, she daily touched what she would never own.

I want to remember the two older women kneeling on large, flat rocks in the river, washing their families' clothes. Though taxis speed by, though tourists have invaded their city, though high-rise hotels have modern washers and driers, many women in Mexico retain the patterns of their mothers. They pound their clothes into the rocks; a picturesque scene, but a difficult life devoid of conveniences.

I want to remember the young boy who at sunset would smooth the beach sand with a long piece of wood. Such a futile task. In a matter of minutes a jogger or a child playing Frisbee would trample the unreal, smooth surface. I tried to imagine his family.

Mouths full of laughter,
the *turistas* come to the tall hotel
with suitcases full of dollars.
Every morning my brother makes
the cool beach sand new for them.
With a wooden board he smooths
away all footprints.

I peek through the cactus fence
and watch the women rub oil
sweeter than honey into their arms and legs
while their children jump
waves or sip drinks from long straws,
coconut white, mango yellow.

Once my little sister
ran barefoot across the hot sand
for a taste.

My mother roared like the ocean,
"No. No. It's their beach.
It's their beach."[1]

So often as tourists we are smiling consumers of fantasy. "Neocolonialists," prolific Professor Stephen Jay Gould calls us.[2] Many citizens of Puerto Vallarta do not enjoy a brunch of assorted juices, fresh fruits, omelettes, beans, sausage, *chilaquiles, pan dulce.* They do not spend their mornings lying in the sun smelling the sweet scent of coconut tanning oil. They do not spend their afternoons wandering from shop to shop buying blouses and silver jewelry. They do not spend their evenings sipping *piña coladas* and listening to *mariachis*. Many Mexicans wake early, go to bed late. Their days and evenings are spent smiling at tourists, catering, serving, cajoling, working, working, working. When they come to the United States seeking a better life for themselves and their families, the exploitation often continues. It exists on both sides of that border.

If the view consumed by most travelers is a distorted one, should travel be abandoned? We humans seem to crave occasional escape from our personal reality. The poet Elizabeth Bishop asks us and herself, "*Is it lack of imagination that makes us come / to imagined places . . .?*"[3] And in another poem,

> Oh, tourist,
> is this how this country is going to answer you
>
> and your immodest demands for a different world,
> and a better life, and complete comprehension
> of both at last . . . ?[4]

Television, movies, quick reads, all transport us from our burdensome dailiness. The danger of snapshots, though, can be snap judgements.

"This is the life," my children would say as they listened to the rhythmic sound of the surf, as they tasted the *ceviche* and *escargot* for the first time. Life in Puerto Vallarta for them was taxi rides and attentive waiters. They quickly looked away from the dark hovels that house so many of the townspeople. That act of looking away is a luxury we cannot ultimately afford. We cannot afford to be lulled.

If travel in Mexico is cheap, it is because resources—including people—are exploited. Behind those smiling brown faces there is anger and resentment. In this unfair world I must, at the very least, respond to the humanity of those trapped in my fantasy lands, all due to an accident of birth. Their reality and the reality of their plight demand my attention.

Though I returned refreshed by the lush beauty of Puerto Vallarta, I also return disturbed, more aware of the frightening disparities in the world, of my good fortune. When I place my photographs of the trip in my family album, I remember the snapshots I didn't take.

Notes

1. Pat Mora, "Fences," in *Communion* (Houston: Arte Público Press, 1991), p. 50.

2. Stephen Jay Gould, review of *African Silences*, by Peter Matthiessen, *New York Times Book Review*, 8 August 1991, p. 29.

3. Elizabeth Bishop, "Questions of Travel," in *Elizabeth Bishop: The Complete Poems 1927–1979* (New York: Farrar, Straus, and Giroux, 1933), p. 94.

4. Elizabeth Bishop, "Arrival at Santos," in *Complete Poems*, p. 89.

II

R E A D I N G   P O E T R Y
I N   P A K I S T A N

It wasn't easy to decide to travel to Pakistan in 1986. I knew that the headlines about terrorists worried my children and parents. But my husband and I had been apart for eight months while he taught at the University of Peshawar through the Fulbright program. I referred to our calls and letters as *mis*communication because the former required shouting and the latter took so long to arrive. Mine is a family of nontravelers, but my husband's urging was persistent. He spent many hours planning a trip for us to India and then back to Pakistan.

At the last moment, my father was hospitalized. He had surgery while we were in Agra. Pictures of the Taj Mahal remind me of my frantic calls home. The time difference and the need to all but scream to be heard made for tense moments. "How's Daddy? How's Daddy?" I would yell into the phone of our hotel room at two in the morning.

In spite of my poor memory, I still remember the flight to Pakistan, the hours spent at London's Heathrow airport, the pep talks I'd give myself on how well I was handling traveling to Asia for the first time, alone. I keep telling my children that learning how to enjoy such solitary trips is important, particularly for women, because we're socialized to feel somehow deficient without a companion.

My excitement began to grow as I saw the Pakistani flight attendants arrive at the boarding gate. They wore a shalwar kameez, a loose, pajamalike, two-piece garment, and a matching head veil, a chador. The music as we boarded, the languages around me, the food served, all assured me that I was indeed going to another continent. I still smile when I remember the Pakistani phrase, "Inshallah [God willing], we shall arrive at eleven o'clock."

By mail, Vern had warned me that I wouldn't be able to see him until I had retrieved my luggage. I remember looking for him in the mob at the Islamabad airport. I remember his huge smile, the hug he'd said he couldn't give in public in a Moslem country.

He was carrying a slender rod on which hung delicate garlands of fresh flowers, white and red, sweet-smelling necklaces. The doorman at the hotel was huge. He wore curly toed shoes, for the tourists I'm sure. Although Vern had bought some outfits for me so that I would not offend anyone by my bare arms or legs, I was stared at constantly, probably because of my uncovered head. What a lesson for a woman who enjoys a friendly glance to suddenly have every man gawking, even in restaurants as I ate. They stared—and stared.

> Horseflies, those eyes
> nipped at my unveiled skin
> day after day, wearied me
> until I, a vain woman,
> avoided mirrors and make-up,
> pulled my hair back
> with one quick twist,
> hid in my wrinkled clothes.[1]

This was particularly true when we arrived in Peshawar, a conservative region in the northwest part of the country, a region of guns, refugees, women hidden in dark burqas. Those full-length cover garments worn in highly traditional households hide a woman literally from head to toes with only a small netted opening for the eyes. How they depressed me. The women seemed so apart, so hidden, wrapped in layers of cloth, and in that oppressive heat. I kept reminding myself of the wise advice of a young Pakistani I'd met in the United States. Her words: "Don't judge."

I was very much looking forward to giving two poetry readings while in Pakistan. The first took place late one afternoon. Our host for this event, a U.S. government official familiar with Pakistani attitudes toward appropriate behavior for women, had invited only females to this gathering and had created a safe, informal setting in his home. He and Vern talked quietly on the margin of our women's web of confidences.

Once inside, the women would drop the chador around their shoulders. None wore a burqa. These were university professors and students, progressive—though they wore the necessary veil. Although this would probably be our only meeting, we chatted openly. During the first few minutes, of course, we were all somewhat reserved, polite, a gathering much like that of women in the United States. Introductions, smiles.

But soon we laughed as women often do when they speak privately. They welcomed my questions, and I welcomed their laughter. We were an island of curiosity. First we talked about some obvious differences. Clothes. They wondered why Western women would even consider being seen in such items as bikinis, why we would embarrass ourselves and our families by such lack of privacy. I wondered aloud why these open, intelligent women would continue to wear a veil.

The answer to my question was complex, as are all answers

about traditions. These women viewed themselves as family symbols and had no desire to shame the family name. Some no longer covered their hair in public, but draped the veil around their shoulders. The chador obviously comforted them: a contrast to our view of that gauzy garment. We too have such symbols to confirm our identity in our particular society, be they jeans, turtlenecks, rings, proper suits. How often do I consider the possibility that women in more repressive societies at times choose their symbols much as I do? They knew, as most educated women around the world know, that many of their customs needed changing to allow women more control over their own lives. In a gentle way, though, they were saying to me, "Be patient. There has been change. Change will continue."

I read poems about women, Mexico, the border, being Mexican American. They'd smile when they'd hear issues and problems much like their own and say, "You are like us." A local poet read poems in a deep voice mournful as a winter wind.

After the reading, we talked again of being women. The young ones spoke of marriage, of hoping to marry a man they chose. They told of women who first saw their spouse in a mirror during their wedding ceremony. I thought of a young, sheltered girl, carefully dressed and adorned. I thought with almost disbelief that in the 1980s a young woman would still look into a mirror to see the face that might rule her life. I thought of that second before she saw her fate; I felt her fear.

My companions spoke of a bride's first visit home, perhaps half a year after marriage, of the tears day after day because she would have to leave again, return to her mother-in-law's. They mentioned the power of that mother-in-law and how generation after generation one group of women oppressed another. Such stories were about small villages, not the women in the room; yet when the father of one of the guests entered, the laughter ceased. Bright women who had but a few moments ago spoken forcefully, now smiled demurely. The professor patted his daughter's head and said to me, "Has she told you that she too writes? Oh, her poems are light, foolish things, of course." He dominated the conversation until he left with his veiled daughter.

The second reading took place in Islamabad near the end of our visit. It was also an afternoon reading. About fifty people attended; three of us read. In the discussions afterward, as well as in a newspaper interview and at a dinner that evening, I noticed considerable interest in my candor about my country. Those asking questions knew about minorities and were curious to know how I was treated. It is difficult to explain our tradition of constructive criticism, our firm belief that we have a responsibility to help our country improve by both stating the changes that we think need to take place and then participating in that change.

After the reading, tea was served. I felt so fortunate to have read in another country with local writers, and to have had careful listeners take an interest in my work. I had the opportunity to talk to a young writer that evening who asked me why I write. When I told her that one of the reasons is to make other women less lonely, because writers have done that for me, she nodded her head with enthusiasm. "That's why I write too," she beamed.

The privilege of giving a poetry reading often includes that bonus of meeting young women brimming with images and energy. She is still with me, part of the memory of women in Pakistan. I wish I could better express my gratitude to such women who infuse me with their spirit in other countries as well as in San Antonio, Laredo, Iowa City, Davidson, and Granville, Ohio. I remember the students taught by my energetic friend Wendy Barker at the University of Texas, San Antonio. I visited their class to answer questions, and then the students read their poems. These were not creative writing students eager to display their wit and erudition as they shredded one another's work. They cared both about language and the writer and gently sought to assist each poem to unfold. I remember their grins when they handed me the gift of a Walt Whitman T-shirt I still own, which their literary group was selling to finance their publication.

I remember the young visual artist in Dallas, a Chicana who had volunteered to meet me at the airport and spend time with me prior to a reading because she liked my work. I couldn't look at her enough. Her eyes and skin shone with her enthusiasm for her students and her work. Shyly she took me to see some of her art pieces on display at the community college where she taught. I remember the African American student at Denison University who had listened intently during my reading. Afterward she grinned at me, "Don't be sad because you have to talk about what needs changing. Look at me. I feel better because you said what I feel."

These women become part of me.

Notes

1. Pat Mora, "Too Many Eyes," in *Communion* (Houston: Arte Público Press, 1991), p. 36.

12

ISLAND IMAGES

The Dominican Republic

One recent winter, rock music fans were singing with the Beach Boys, "Aruba, Jamaica, ooo I want to take ya." As we pull on coats and gloves during cold, gray months, daydreams of warm sand and the turquoise Caribbean lure us. Escape to islands, of course, has perennial appeal. Movies, television, and tempting ads teach us that islands are great pleasure platters offering smiling and respectful natives, inexpensive shopping sprees, romance beneath whispering palms.

Like all cameras, those recording island images are selectively placed. And in our weaker moments, we're grateful for the deception. Far easier to counter a pale winter sun with thoughts of Bermuda and the Bahamas than to confront the more troublesome aspects of the Caribbean and islands not on the Beach Boys' list: Haiti, the Dominican Republic.

My initial reaction on my visit to the latter was excitement as the plane descended into Santo Domingo. Such a stark contrast between the severity of the Chihuahuan desert where I lived and the wonder of green patches surrounded by an ocean lively with countless shades of blue. I soon began to see the unglamorous reality of the region: unpainted shacks; puddles of black water; thin, barefoot children with outstretched hands.

Because of my interest in cultural conservation, I spent the first days visiting cultural agencies and museums. I was also taken to the first cathedral in the Americas, to the home that belonged to the family of Christopher Columbus. I met an enthusiastic anthropologist very committed to issues of national identity who had started a series of Sunday morning workshops—*talleres infantiles,* she called them. The workshops were led by master teachers with proficiency in some aspect of cultural expression, or *cultural manifestations,* a term this anthropologist preferred to *folklore.* But the television set in my hotel room revealed the challenge of preserving Dominican culture. The set had more U.S. channels than my set at home. In a Spanish-speaking country, I was hearing ads for sales in Chicago, watching the current season of "Cheers," and reruns of "Hogan's Heroes"—all in English. One of my hosts took me to Tropiburger, a Dominican version of the Golden Arches, an example of what my companion called "transculturation."

Candid museum professionals voiced their concern that their fellow Dominicans fear angering the United States. "We are psychologically so dependent on you," said one. "Many Dominicans want the freedom to visit your country for many reasons—visits to doctors, for example. It's a status symbol to have a doctor in the United States. We fear that open talk of nationalism may mean visa problems." Other Dominicans nodded their agreement. With deep reluctance many do decide to journey to the United States, discouraged by the almost daily power failures, the frightening inflation. Many return with our dollars and build homes they visit once a year, cars that sit untouched. These absent Dominicans are referred to ruefully as "Dominican jerks" by those stubbornly determined to improve life in their country.

My ultimate destination was Plan Sierra, a rural development project in the central mountain range. The pilot project is a model for reducing poverty in a deforested area while restoring the ecosystem. The project includes rural health clinics, management of existing forests, a technical assistance program for isolated communities, and the preparation of a new generation of Dominicans who understand ecological concepts.

The main office of Plan Sierra is located in the small community of San José de Las Matas. I arrived at night. The stars seemed huge, because the only light on the winding road came from the headlights of our jeep. How eerie to see people walking in darkness. My first night was my first experience with mosquito netting, which succeeded in keeping my hungry, buzzing companions from my skin. But the night was a noisy one. Motorbikes zoomed around the block right up until the time the roosters started. I never heard those braggarts again. Every subsequent evening I was too exhausted from jarring jeep rides and long walks to isolated communities.

Each day program directors took me to different sites to help me understand the scope of Plan Sierra. I felt heavy with our U.S. abundance, embarrassed by the thoughtfulness and generosity of the people who greeted us with tiny cups of black coffee thick with sugar. One elderly gentleman who had walked a mile down a "road" that looked like a rock-strewn, washed-out riverbed took my arm to guide me back to his isolated community. "*Ay, señora, que vergüenza que no tenemos camino y que tenga usted que andar. Yo le ayudo,*" he said solicitously. "How embarrassed we are that we don't have a road and that you must walk. I'll help you." He told me that he was the treasurer of the school committee and that when he asked his fellow community members for funds, they knew they had to dig into their pockets. The school was a bare room with rough benches. The only light came through the windows and door.

Each day at Plan Sierra I witnessed what we seldom see in island images: what can't be bought. I watched a field worker gently and respectfully discuss nutrition with a frail, elderly couple, their clothes patched, their hands cut and calloused from weaving thatch and perhaps earning one dollar day after day. In a tiny house, high in the mountains, I watched the project staff work as partners with a community struggling to become self-sufficient. They greeted us with fresh fruit, then sat us down and began a series of formal presentations that they had prepared for us. A young woman spoke eloquently about why she and her teenage friends needed a soccer ball. She was a natural leader, bright and articulate, and there she was making a plea before her community for a ball. Even breakfast before the two-hour walk to school is a luxury for some in those mountains.

One day we stopped to watch a family pounding thick sticks with two hands into a shallow river. "They're looking for gold," my companion said. "They will pound like that all day."

> The grandmother's damp clothes
> cling to legs thinner than the sticks she plunges.
> Her fingers, hungry snakes, slide
> through the trapped water poised for a glint.[1]

I watched the exhilaration of the staff at seeing farmers and their families proudly show me their mininurseries, tiny pines and coffee plants: hope. Every staff member spoke to me about how important their work was, the director, the cook. Occasionally, one woman would question me about my country. "You have so much," she would say, barely containing her anger. "It is your responsibility to set a good example, to lead."

Near the end of my trip, I met Doña Ana in Puerto Plata. She wanted to tell me about a house for street children that she had started. We sat in two rocking chairs, listening to the wind rush through palm fronds and bang wooden window shutters.

Rain began to pelt the house and electricity vanished. In the dark we rocked with only a bit of candlelight. I've tried to write a poem about Doña Ana but have never quite succeeded, probably because I know what I want to say, which never bodes well for poems that are journeys to the unknown. Doña Ana is one of those grand older women I love, her voice worn like an old familiar record, the voice of storytellers.

She told me about the clothes store she had owned, located across the street from the police compound. Every afternoon, before the tourist boat arrived with its load of eager shoppers, the police would round up the street children so that the *turistas* would not be bothered by tugs and small open palms. I had seen areas in which some of these children lived, houses made of cardboard, magazine pictures taped on the "walls" for decoration, "streets" that were *agua negra,* black water and sewage. I had also seen the elaborate tourist hotels on the beach, well removed from one aspect of the island's reality. Doña Ana remembered how all afternoon the children had to stand in the compound, in the glare of the island sun. From her store she would hear the whimpers and cries. The beatings. The police ignored her, "Please, please don't hit them. They're children," and so she convinced other women to help her buy a small house where the children could hide and rest from the heat.

A widow now, she talked about her husband's blindness before he died and how she had rails of pipe placed throughout their large house as hand paths, his labyrinth of safety. At eighty-seven she opened a house for *ancianos,* the elderly with no place to go. We rocked, listening to the rain. I reveled in being in the presence of such an improviser. Doña Ana said she was recovering from surgery so was not as active as usual. Carefully she handed me the rose-colored fish and gold trees she was making from tiny seashells. *"Regalitos para mis muchachas y muchachos."* "Small gifts for my girls and boys."

Because I'd spent my life on the U.S.-Mexican border, I felt prepared for Dominican poverty. I wasn't. I also felt prepared to be inspired by those who invest their lives in the service of their land and of others. The surprise of the trip was that I was more than inspired. I was startled, as startled as by the green lizards walking slowly on office walls.

Over and over I asked myself: Why? We are startled by the unexpected, the unfamiliar. As a society, and more and more as a world, we have agreed to focus our attention on the personal: personal pleasure, personal prestige, personal power. The planet and its people are a set of vacation options, not a responsibility or an inheritance. "It's money that matters," sings Randy Newman.

While working to preserve the hydraulic potential of their country, the staff at Plan Sierra produce energy on a daily basis—human energy. I wonder if in our determination to be comfortable, entertained, and insulated, we deny ourselves more inspired and inspiring lives, choose lives in which unselfishness and nobility surprise us.

Notes

1. Pat Mora, "Dominican Gold," in *Communion* (Houston: Arte Público Press, 1991), p. 58.

13

A HAZE IN GUATEMALA

Visiting a Latin American country usually means the opportunity to speak Spanish, a pleasure I miss in Cincinnati. Such travel also means the opportunity to hear cab drivers say with pride, "*Este es el país mas lindo del mundo.*" "This is the most beautiful country in the world." I smile when we hear the now familiar phrase as we leave the airport at Guatemala City, *la capital*.

The first days we are burdened by trunks and heavy boxes, which hold my husband's archeological equipment. I hear porters who help us move the cumbersome objects laugh to one another, "*¿Y a quién tienen en estas cajas?*" "Who's in these boxes anyway?" It is far easier finally to forget the inconveniences of the equipment than it is to forget the stories of repression, torture, and murder in these rugged mountains. Our guides assure us that these are exaggerated stories from the past, that an army base has now been built in every area of the country to ensure peace and order. I ponder the difference in our concept of the military. Do those very visible uniforms and machine guns held casually by young men who look about fourteen years of age really comfort people? Those who hold stories of human cruelty within them carry that burden with every step.

The duality, or, more accurately, complexity, of surface natural beauty—volcanic lakes, the hum of rain forests—and unseen suffering is part of life.

Unfortunately, sound bites and head shots delude us into superficial generalities. Life is more predictable if all police are evil, all poets pure. Over and over I'm surprised by the mix we are as individuals and countries. I assumed that Holy Week in a Latin American country, for example, would be a sober, solemn time. Stores throughout Guatemala City were closed. I had images of filled churches. And indeed many devout Christians did attend services, did reflect on the religious significance of those days, but many also viewed the time as a holiday. Because festivals lure tourists, Holy Week is a boon to merchants in the colonial city of Antigua, once the capital of Guatemala. Early on the morning of Good Friday, the residents begin to cover the cobblestone streets with carpets of flowers. Now colored saw-dust—gold, deep turquoise, magenta, purple—is also used for the intricate designs, as well as pine needles and palm blooms, pale yellow slivers of fresh scent. We watch townspeople bending to complete their designs with purple and yellow mums. Fresh ginger glows like dark red votives bordering one family's effort. They sprinkle their ephemeral art, and for a moment the air is sweet. Perhaps we stare at these plush carpets in awe because we know that the procession is on its way, winding through the town, stepping rhythmically on these lovely designs, leaving crushed faint colors on these streets.

Making a carpet or bearing one of the wooden platforms on which statues from the church are carried is a way of showing devotion, of giving thanks, of requesting forgiveness, of showing respect. In the morning procession, the prominent statue is Christ carrying the cross. Men dress either as Romans with helmets, breast plates, and whips, or in long purple garments with white head coverings and spears. Incense drifts through the crowd. After statues of Christ comes the band, trumpets and drums, men in suits, a number also wearing jaunty baseball caps. This group is followed by women, heads covered with *mantillas,* who carry statues of Mary. Like the day, the procession is a mix of the solemn and the commercial. The procession incongruously becomes a parade and ends with marchers selling balloons and cotton candy.

I hear the tourist next to me say she came seeking answers, which is what I guess we're all seeking. Travelers are in a land in the middle, between their own country and the country they seek to understand. The tourist's husband died five years ago, after forty years of marriage, and for the first time in her life, she says, she sleeps alone—no sister, roommate, husband, just she and the noises. She says she volunteered for everything, but her life feels empty. She watches the statues and says she needs a big change. Why do we come?

All day, as the procession winds through the town, residents and tourists wander, buy, eat, laugh. In an almost empty church, an elderly woman lovingly strokes the blood-covered legs of a beaten Christ, whispers to the statue. In the courtyard women from nearby indigenous communities sell their weaving. Three young girls wearing *cortes,* traditional long skirts, jump rope. Two slap the rope and one runs in, holds her skirt as she jumps faster and faster, runs out to check on a possible customer, runs back into the rope's spin. Across the street, two white-haired women sit in a doorway slowly unwrapping tamales, their picnic. The quiet fiesta is everywhere.

At noon some townspeople go to church, but as the priest forcefully and solemnly laments people's lack of moral courage, outside, spirits are high. Laughter rises like balloons. At three, churches fill. With much pageantry, Christ is removed from the cross. The whir of drums and *matracas,* noisemakers, fills the air. A young woman next to me explains: "It rained and stormed when He was taken from the cross." The second procession of the day begins. This time the men wear black and the statue of Christ lies in a gold and glass case. Churches empty, tourists begin to drift away, merchants compare their sales to last year's profits.

Whether driving from Guatemala City to Antigua or to the market at Chichicastenango, we pass small, dark dwellings with rusty roofs, cabbage fields and pine trees, women stretching red and blue clothes to dry in the grass, their weaving like small carpets on the hills. I think of rural women walking to the river or lake in Mexico, India, and now Guatemala. They scrub clothes, they carry water on their heads, rhythms rippling back through the centuries. I watch them splashing water onto their crops, on their knees tossing rainwater caught in small cisterns onto onions, potatoes, watermelons.

At the market I hear words I do not understand, for more than half of the country is indigenous, many speaking their native languages. Whether in Peru, Mexico, or Guatemala, indigenous populations—their distinctive clothes, music, weaving—are good for tourism, but tourism—or we—exploits them. We mail their pictures on postcards they will never see to countries they will never visit. How easily their cultures become commodities that we use to decorate our homes. We know how to purchase and collect objects. How much harder it is to take the time to learn from people who may not look like us or sound like us.

At the church that is said to be a blend of Christianity and indigenous beliefs, two little girls offer to be our guides, to tell us what people pray for in different parts of the church, bringing candles, rose petals, incense, liquor as offerings, here for health, here for fertility, here for a good harvest. The girls open their palms and look at us, ready to dart away with money in their fists. Outside I hear Quiché, not Spanish, on the church's loudspeaker. The market seems everywhere, women with *sutes,* folded head cloths, the mix of weaving and flowers. A man staggers toward me, his eyes glazed. I move aside, but turn to watch him walk away. Blood. I see blood matted on the back of his head. A fresh red gash. Did he fall or was he pushed? Does he know he's bleeding? The price of curiosity, wanting to see and yet not wanting to see, or maybe knowing that I'll never really see.

We fly to Tikál, Guatemala's most famous Mayan ruin, located in the area known as the Petén. Over and over I notice that the Guatemalans and Mexicans swimming and playing at the more expensive hotels don't have dark skin. The hierarchy of color is worldwide. We visit small nearby towns, see horses cooling their hoofs in the lake, a traffic sign that shows a crocodile crossing the road, a white church whose domes say Spaniards, Moors. A boom box blares a rap song, "Let's get down, get, get, get, get down." In a bookstore I see Barbie's story in Spanish, *El Hombre Araña*—Spider Man, and Yogey Bear—*El Oso Yogui*. I ask about children's books of local legends or myths. I walk out empty handed. On the road we are stopped and asked for our papers by patrolling military. I feel my skin. We drive on, nervous. *Ninfeas,* water plants, bloom purple, healthy, while next to them children play in the dirt without the opportunity to thrive. I see lone trees high on hilltops, bare survivors of human need and greed, reminders of the grandeur of surviving, of stubbornly weathering the unexpected and rising, rising.

The vegetation as we approach the rain forest becomes more and more dense. We stop to look at the pink blossoms of the *árbol de matrimonio,* wedding tree, and at the intricate nests made by the *oropéndula,* a noisy bird whose tail feathers flash yellow in flight. Their nests hang like intricately woven gloves swaying in the branches of a huge tree. Our guide, Félix, laughs when he points out a tree he says is called *palo de gringo,* "gringo tree," because the bark peels like skin burned by the sun. He tells us that on May third some communities celebrate *el Día de la Cruz*, "the Day of the Cross." People erect crosses in front of their homes and decorate them with apples, bananas, mangoes. Children come to adore the cross. They genuflect before it and are allowed to take a fruit. "Of course," he says, "you know how children are. They go collecting from house to house."

I hear an archaeologist refer to local guides as *conocedores*, knowledgeable ones, which is what Félix is. Steadily he's showing us his world, the birds and plants. He shows me faint scars on a *sapote*, gum tree. Bags to collect the resin are hung beneath the cuts that spiral up the tree. I begin to notice the trees wherever I walk, the wounds as commonplace as erosion. At Tikál we walk toward the pyramids, studying the rain forest around us. The red trunk of a tree could be the webbed foot of a dinosaur. A lone egret stares into the distance, a white silence in the cicadas' whir. Epiphytes, air plants, fur branches. Leaves gossip, their green tongues warm in the afternoon sun. Irrepressible roots crawl the land's hard surface seeking water in the dry season. Moss called *velo de novia*, wedding veil, curls and sways high in the breeze. To Félix, Tikál means "place of the voices" and refers to the acoustics and echoes. In any site that humans built long ago, I like to think their voices linger, faint, undecipherable, but in the air. Félix comes to Tikál often but enjoys our awe at the pyramids that soar into the jungle canopy. "We'll come and see the sun rise on top of Temple 4," he says.

As we leave the hotel before daybreak, car lights flash on a band of youngsters silently getting off a bus. Gardeners, I'm told. They look about twelve years old. Félix knows his way in the dark, finally stopping the bumpy ride on hard limestone at the base of a hill. With little enthusiasm for climbing a pyramid, I look up and see not steps ascending steeply but a series of ladders attached to rocks scaling the tallest pre-Hispanic structure in the New World. Nothing in Félix's attitude suggests I have a choice. I glare at my husband and start up, ladder after ladder. I don't trust my body like they seem to trust theirs. Every time my companions tell me I'm almost there, I stifle a scream of annoyance. And, of course, I'm also thinking of the trip down, backward.

We reach the top and sit in silence. Swallows dart into the door frame behind us. It's cloudy, so the sunrise will be gradual rather than dramatic. We sit and look down on the trees, see the roof combs of the other temples in the distance, white limestone testimony of humans who erected these monumental stages for their pageantry. I think of the minds who designed these thrusts of rock. Then the temples were painted red, black, yellow, blue, green. Priests with massive feather headdresses paraded high above the believing crowd. In A.D. 750, eighty thousand Maya lived in the area. They assembled down below, incense drifted up the temple steps. Musicians played drums and blew their warm breath into shells.

My companions gently begin to talk to me, to show me what they see. "There," they say. Parrots fly by, always in pairs. Some distance away, toucans land into a bare tree, become its black decorations, *crrrrrrk, crrrrrrk*. Birds screech, chirp, squeak, and whistle, the sounds thickening as light spreads over the leaves. Howler monkeys begin their odd roaring, and occasionally a woodpecker drums. The sun appears, a white host shimmering in the sky. Félix says the animals are happy at the sun's return, and I wonder if indeed they open their mouths for the pleasure of raising their voices, of releasing what was hushed at night. I wonder about humans raising our voices, about the joy of our own sound rising, of those humans denied that pleasure.

In my few days in Guatemala, I strained to see. I saw rivers of clouds wander through *barrancas,* deep canyons, the purple blooms of jacaranda, erosion everywhere, women holding children. *"Dos manos mas para trabajar."* "Two more hands for working." Lake Atitlán hid in mist, as did volcanos day after day. Although Guatemala is said to have thirty-three of them, I never clearly saw one. I knew their presence and shape, caught glimpses of their sides and cones, but fog, clouds, mist, incense, and smoke from smoldering fields produced a haze throughout my stay. Perhaps that lack of clarity is part of Guatemala, a country obscured from our total vision.

14

ESCRIBE, ESCRIBE

From the moment I boarded the Cubana jet at the Toronto airport, Russia's presence in Cuba was evident. "Look at the odd printing on all the signs," I heard people whispering. *Communists.* I squirmed some in my seat. After all, I'm a good child of the fifties. My grandmothers and aunts probably believed that all *comunistas* had red eyes. I craved protection my first night in Havana.

The inspection at the Havana airport was slow and tedious. Because this was my first visit to a communist country, I was apprehensive. Even my unused yellow writing tablets were shaken to insure that subversive material was not hidden between the pages. I suppressed a moan when an official chastised my chosen roommate for carrying mail addressed to political prisoners. Great, I thought. Why didn't she warn me? Now our every move will be monitored. I began seeing melodramatic black-and-white spy-movie scenarios. Then another surprise. Before the bus left the airport, an official collected our passports. Now how would I prove my identity? It was midnight. The streets were dark, deserted. I felt alone and somehow without a country.

That first night was one of those flexibility tests that convince the comfort-seeking to hug the hearth. The beach cottages were scattered along dark streets, the promised ocean was nowhere in sight, the small, bare rooms produced groans of disappointment, the kitchen strengthened diet resolves, our luggage had yet to appear. Two weeks, I thought. Can I make it?

The heat the following morning was oppressive. In December. And the lectures began, also hot. Tour guides, journalists, lawyers, academics, government officials all sang the same song: "We like Americans but not the U.S. administration. It abuses its small neighbor located a mere ninety miles from Florida." Reluctantly I became accustomed to the labels *imperialistic, exploitive, bourgeoisie*.

Within the first few days, however, we realized that we were far safer on the streets of Havana than on the streets of Houston. Although flirtation is a national sport, physical aggression against women is not tolerated. What an irony to feel secure strolling Havana streets with female friends at 11:00 P.M. when so many friends and relatives had admonished me to "be careful in Cuba."

The topic of this travel seminar in the late eighties was political communication in Cuba. Among our presenters were officials from the Cuban Institute of Friendship for Peoples of the World, the Union of Cuban Jurists, and the editorial staff of the official party newspaper, *Granma*. Daily presentations were complemented by ballet and folklore troupe performances and by visits to the U.S. Interest Section, museums, and a cigar factory.

One afternoon our group was taken to visit a Catholic home for the elderly. Obviously Cuba was officially saying, "Notice: the Church is alive and well." A white-garbed nun dutifully greeted us as a choir of frail singers practiced somewhat squeakily in the chapel. Predictable political maneuvers. Yet the afternoon lingers. The images. The smiling, curious, white-haired women who drifted toward me, surrounded me like curious pigeons, kissed my hands, stroked my clothes, whispered, "*¿De dónde eres? De dónde eres?*" "Where are you from?" Such open faces.

And oh their joy when I said, "*Soy de los Estados Unidos.*" "I am from the United States." Their whispers confided conspiratorially that many were from Spain—that they liked Americans much more than Russians. Sounds my beloved aunt, Mexican-born yet fiercely "North American," would have made. Here I was in Cuba surrounded by her contemporaries. A balding woman in a wheelchair stopped me. She proudly wore a small orchid behind each ear. "*¡Qué bonita!*" I said, bending close to her face. "How lovely you look." "*Era,*" she countered. "I was once." Only the sight of a uniformed guard marred the visit. Why a uniform in a home for the elderly? we wondered. But uniforms abound in Cuba.

Probably the question I'm most frequently asked about this trip is: Did I see The Man? Yes, although all credit goes to Magda, my determined friend. She is a New Yorker and not easily daunted. Somehow she succeeded in securing a press pass, in having our cameras inspected in the crush of reporters, and in wrangling a much-coveted invitation. Such spunk. There we were on the foreign press bus, en route to Castro's inauguration of a film school. The international coverage was considerable, and buses were jammed for the ride to the outlying community of San Antonio de los Baños. Was I really going to see Castro?

Diplomatic dignitaries began to arrive at the outdoor gathering. In true revolutionary style, a special section had been reserved in front for the workers who had constructed the new site. Excitement mounted. Clapping began, and suddenly white birds were released. They swirled above the crowd as the stage party appeared. And there *they* were. Fidel Castro and Gabriel

García Márquez, "Gabo" as Castro called him. Two Latinos who continue to create history, political and literary. Castro moved into the audience and began to shake the hands of the eighty-one students from twenty-four countries who constituted the first film class.

And how the Cubans respond to Castro. Next to me was a pregnant woman fretting audibly about her view of the stage. "Oh, no," she lamented, "that large man is going to block my view of Fidel." Fidel is their hero. We seldom see such adulation of a political figure in our country, but then Castro does not have to contend with critical journalists or, in fact, with any negative publicity. The workers around me, all proudly wearing a red scarf distributed as a memento of the event, beamed as they looked up at him. And finally, after the preliminary speeches, after an elaborate introduction, the khakied father figure moved to the mike. Cameras flashed and flashed. Like sunflowers, we became an assembly of craned necks.

Castro was mellow, joking, gently stroking his gray moustache, playing the crowd. As my friend Magda observed, he was Castro the myth maker, describing what he labeled the "symphony of work" that had produced the structure around us, the "music of hammers and saws." He praised not only Cubans' national pride but now their international pride in creating a school for the new cinema of the entire Third World, a school destined, he said, to last as long as the revolution—which is destined to last for eternity. The crowd beamed.

It was intriguing to be in the midst of such palpable devotion. As memorable as Castro, however, were two Cubans who are not famous. In spite of the severe heat, I had repeatedly visited a medicinal herb store I'd spied on my first walk down Obispo Street. The shop would be either closed or crowded with customers who quickly called out their requests: *canita santa, romero, botón de oro, sassafrás.* Finally, one afternoon I found the owner, Don Jaime, alone. I've learned not to be too aggressive with traditional healers. Because they have been bruised by cynics, they are protective of their knowledge. I took my time, said I was interested in such herb lore in the Southwest and was likewise curious about his supplies. I started jotting down names. Don Jaime watched me out of the corner of his eyes as customers straggled in. Somehow I passed the test. *"Escribe, escribe."* "Write, write," he said eventually, and began naming each plant on the counter. "This is good propaganda," he said. "Be sure to write about these natural cures. Don't forget." A man with a mission.

Though I didn't share this with my generous host, I am as fascinated by the faith involved in traditional healing as I am in the herbs and roots themselves. From the *monte* near his home and with the assistance of other herb gatherers, he stated that he could offer his customers relief from migraines, ulcers, heart and kidney ailments, asthma, flu, rashes, and pimples. He could prescribe *romero* to cure baldness and *gengibre* to "increase sexual prowess." He was less willing to discuss items popular in *brujeria,* witchcraft. A tall woman watched him lean over the counter to check my spelling. She winked at me and said, *"Don Jaime, dile de los baños."* "Don Jaime, tell her about the baths. Tell her about boiling these plants for a cleansing."

Don Jaime quickly hobbled to the other end of the counter. Subject of witchcraft closed. Yes, he hobbled. It was hard to suppress a grin at this most sincere man determinedly selling his cures although he had an injured foot, a lisp, small facial lesions, a damaged ear, a hacking cough.

"Do these cures work?" I asked when I'd taken many notes. "Oh, yes," he said. "Why I haven't seen a doctor in twenty years and just look at me." Look at him I do, because he reveled in posing for my camera. And I remember him with gratitude and deep affection. Like so many Cubans I met, he took his work seriously. Money was not his motivator.

Don Jaime

In the pale tangle of light and leaf,
rocks and pebbles tumble,
ringing in the dawn like clay bells
as Don Jaime shuffles down the *monte*
glowing and dew-drenched as verbena
and salvia that curl around the lattice
of his fingers, wild cures sprouting roots
in the loam of his palms. The lame healer
and his grandson drag their basket brimming
with the rustle of branches and bark,
with *botón de oro,* flowers yellow as canaries,
the hot perfume an irresistible honey,
dizzying butterflies that doze
on the bodies and basket of this harvest
of faith, on these hands brimming
with ancient teas, pale green steam
which if inhaled with closed eyes
make us wonder
where we've been.[1]

There is a saying in Spanish, *No hay mal que por bien no venga.* The gist of these words is: it's an ill wind that blows no good. Indeed. Because we were unable to use our credit cards in Cuba, I met a delightful woman.

Our dependence on plastic money became evident soon after our arrival in Havana. Because U.S. banks do not honor Cuban receipts, U.S. credit cards are non-negotiable. How frustrated we were to see credit cards issued in other countries accepted by clerks and waiters, as our meals changed from *pollo, arroz, y plátanos fritos*—chicken, rice, and fried bananas—to bags of popcorn and slices of pizza.

Like any assertive (and hungry) U.S. North Americans, my companions and I were determined to find a solution. Because neither our hotel nor local travel agencies yielded success, one evening we walked to a bank. The line was long and the pace slow, but we foolishly hoped for a cash advance. Cubans are far more patient in such lines than we are. I began chatting with the woman in front of me. She was in her early sixties and had retired recently but was finding housework far more never-ending than her job had been. (Sound familiar?) I asked about holiday celebrations, because I had seen only one spindly looking Christmas tree in Havana.

"Oh I'll have my family over, of course," she said. Her smile grew. "My children and grandchildren love the meal I'll fix— pork, good rice, and my special *arroz con leche* [rice pudding]."

"Tell me how you make it," I said, savoring the moment of talking recipes in Cuba in December. She shared her secrets with great relish, right down to the slivers of lemon peel.

Eventually I reached the front of the line and had my request rejected. I returned to the dark street a bit dispirited, finally convinced that my credit cards would get a good rest for two weeks.

"Psssst," someone said from the shadows in front of the bank. I turned. There stood my dainty Cuban recipe sharer. "Where are you going to eat dinner?" she asked. "I mean, you said you needed money. You need to eat you know. You can come to my house. I'll feed you."

Such a moment. "Oh, no, *Señora,*" I said. "I'm doing fine, but thank you so very much for inviting me."

She paused. "Well, wouldn't you have done that for me if I had been a guest in your country?"

I wonder.

A certain missionary fervor characterized many of the Cubans who took this desert Latina in as a sister. The fervor was impressive, as was the determination of this small country to provide access to movies, museums, sports events, educational opportunities, and health care. Revolutionary. How could I not be impressed by a free baseball game attended by sixty thousand, by a massive research hospital to which any patient could be referred, by a national system of neighborhood-based preventive health care, by huge youth camps designed to introduce uniformed "pioneers" to career options? With substantial aid from the then U.S.S.R., the revolution has "triumphed" in requiring a population to abandon consumerism for the welfare of the whole. The vast changes in Russia, of course, have us wondering what will happen in Cuba.

The price for unity? "Within the Revolution, everything; against the Revolution, nothing." The price is too high for those of us who need freedom of speech no less than we need oxygen. However, this trip allowed me to reflect on the commitment of revolutionaries as opposed to our comfortable complacency, to reflect with some dismay on our embarrassing greed, and to reflect on the value of human interactions as opportunities for learning. In this media age we are bombarded by images that others select as accurate. Travel provides the luxury of drawing our own conclusions, of meeting fellow humans and being gently reminded of our similarities.

Cuba is soft green hills, an ocean clear and gentle. Cuba is blue, pink, and yellow balconies, arches that, though in disrepair, whisper of Spaniards who settled on this island of banana trees, bougainvillea, sea pines. Although Cuba is no longer a Soviet presence, Cuba remains *la revolución,* government-controlled newspapers and airwaves, the freedom to agree. Cuba is standing in line for wonderful *guayaba,* mango, or eggnog ice cream at Copellia's, chatting with ever-friendly Cubans about the fabled United States while an anti-American rally is taking place, reportedly attended by eighty thousand. Cuba is paper shortages and vintage fifties cars. Cuba is a now-empty plaza above which banners of Che flap to the music of a grand piano, old songs, remnants of a bygone time when Hemingway drank daiquiris and *mojitos* with his *compañeros,* his companions. Cuba is the Havana Libre that was once the Havana Hilton, a country of slogans. Fidel.

But Cuba is more than Fidel, as all countries are more than the personalities who symbolize them. I smile when I remember our bright and determined guide Lilia laughing with us and saying, "Just because I'm a Communist doesn't mean I don't have a sense of humor." I fondly remember Pepe, a lithographer, who came from the fields to the city twenty-five years ago and has made art *his* proper work for the revolution. "Drawing is the only thing I know how to do well," he said to me, his eyes playful, peering over his glasses. "I love it." On my last visit to his shop, he said, "Here. Isn't this your favorite piece?" He held a print I'd longed to give my husband, fronds around a stone mask, mysterious, a hint of voodoo. Over and over I had held up the piece. But I couldn't afford it. "It's yours," he said smiling straight into my eyes.

Cuba is a complex social system of interest to economists, political scientists, health care professionals. But for me, Cuba is people.

Notes

1. Pat Mora, "Don Jaime," in *Communion* (Houston: Arte Público Press, 1991), p. 21.

15

POET AS *CURANDERA*

Ultima, the wise *curandera* in Rudolfo Anaya's novel *Bless Me Ultima*, was my first encounter with these traditional healers. I grew up in a middle-class home and neighborhood, and though the aunt and grandmother who lived with us were quick to brew herb teas for all ailments, they were also quick to visit doctors when necessary.

Soon after talking about Ultima with a community college night class, I taught a student at a university campus who wrote an essay about a *bruja,* a witch. I was just beginning to spend time writing when I read his paper. Because I was fascinated by the student's story, I asked him to come to my office and tell me more about the woman he had described who lived on the outskirts of El Paso. Although I never met her, she is the woman in my poem *"Bruja:* Witch." I remain intrigued by a woman who can "stretch into the long free wings" of an owl, who can "fly into the night," who can "tilt and dip and soar."[1]

I began listening to stories about *brujas* and *curanderas* and to read what I could find. I wrote my only short story, "Hands," published by Arte Público Press on this theme. Certainly the belief in witchcraft is not merely a historical fact. Even in this scientific age, some men, and probably more women, in Mexico and in Mexican American communities continue to seek solutions in the occult, some even frantically follow the prescriptions of a feared being. A rich topic tugs at the subconscious. Black magic. Dark forces difficult to control. Sexual power. Anthropologist Ruth Behar, in writing about the power of witchcraft during the time of the Inquisition in Mexico, notes what is no less true today of women who believe in magical powders. "While placing herbs and powders in the food they served to their husbands, or bringing eggs to a ligature, may seem to be trivial means of exercising power, in fact the real stakes were political, given that women's ultimate aim was to control and change the behavior of the men who dominated them."[2] Some have written of the poet as witch, as *bruja,* as one who knows eerie secrets and who can manipulate words as she gazes at the world with frightening eyes.

My primary interest, though, is in *curanderas* who use a gentler power, *magic,* if you will. I think of her.

> Like a large black bird, she feeds on
> the desert, gathering herbs for her basket.
> Her days are slow, days of grinding
> dried snake into powder, of crushing
> wild bees to mix with white wine.[3]

Like any Chicana writer, I could speak at length about the frustrations of witnessing to our culture. The healing process that takes place at a successful poetry reading, though, can be one of the benefits that sends me back to the oh-so-blank sheets of paper. *Abuelita,* "grandmother," poems seem to cast spells perhaps because *abuelitas* do.

The new mother cries with her baby
in the still desert night,
sits on the dirt floor of the two-room house,
rocks the angry bundle
tears sliding down her face.

The *abuelita* wakes, shakes her head,
finds a dried red chile
slowly shakes the wrinkled pod
so the seeds rattle

$\qquad\qquad\qquad$ ts . ss, ts . ss.

The *abuelita*

$\qquad\qquad\qquad$ ts. ss, ts . ss

gray-haired shaman

$\qquad\qquad\qquad$ ts . ss, ts . ss

cures her two children

$\qquad\qquad\qquad$ ts . ss

with sleep[4]

Note the elements: learned wisdom, ritual, solutions spring-
ing from the land. All are essential to *curanderas,* who listen
to voices from the past and the present, who evolve from their
culture. Discussions of holistic medicine, of integration of mind
and body, reaffirm that definitions of illness and wellness are
culture bound. We might consider it essential to stay in our
comfortable homes or apartments if the soles of our feet were
covered with blisters. The migrant worker, however, might sigh,
apply a salve, and trudge from field to field. Illness is both a
biological and social reality, and our reactions are learned. An
Anglo grandmother might give her grandson a pink spoonful
of over-the-counter medication for a stomach ache, whereas a

Mexican grandmother might fix the boy a cup of hot *hierba-buena,* mint tea. Familiar rituals.

Both women have knowledge of a particular lore. Emphasis on holistic medicine makes us more keenly aware that psychological healing is as important as caring for biological wounds. Although our age is uncomfortable with the concept of magic, we know that often in life our senses confirm a reality we do not understand. We ingest a medication and pain eases, tension subsides; we are refreshed and able to respond to our surroundings with more of our total being. In like manner, we sometimes read or listen to words that enter us and alter our mood, change our perceptions.

The indigenous healer has always known this. Steeped in cultural traditions, she uses the familiar for healing. She has her patients use roses, candles, eggs, lemons, garlic, geraniums— items not foreign to her clients and also within their means. She emphasizes using basic elements: boiling flowers, crushing bees, grinding herbs.

A Chicana poet also uses elements of commonality with her listeners: the importance of family, the retelling of familiar tales. The *curandera* incorporates her herbal lore and her attention to the subtle changes in her natural world with traditions and stories of her people. She learns her healing craft not in a traditional medical program but informally, orally, much as many Chicana writers are part of an oral, storytelling tradition. Often without formal creative writing training, we struggle to preserve what has given solace in the past. The triumph over cruelty and injustice related in poems and stories can be a shared triumph for an audience, a healing confirmation.

In the poem "1910," Doña Luz walks "on the black / beams and boards; still smoking, / that had been Upton's Five-and-Dime." Upton was a man who called his Mexican customers "Thieves. All thieves."[5] Because Mexican culture values collectivism over emphasis on the individual, perhaps the group experience of confronting what are often private sorrows has particular value.

Like the *curandera,* then, the writer creates an informal atmosphere conducive to holistic healing—the healing of affirmation, of identification, of confirmation, of wholeness. In a supportive climate, the listener can confront a reality much as she would an ugly wound and yet experience relief; the known and named is far more bearable than the unspoken and feared. Obviously, there is no guarantee that the ritual, whether *una limpiesa,* a ritual cleansing by a *curandera,* or listening to a series of poems, will ease a pain, but I'm intrigued by the possibility. Faith is essential.

When the silence about a culture ends, the words pour out, often loud and angry. "Survival is expensive," a *curandero* says. "Sometimes I wish I were like everyone else." Minority writers, and all writers, know that feeling. I want more Chicanas to write, but I know the discouragement that awaits them. We live in a society that neither values nor respects what we do. Those close to writers wonder why they invest so much of their time and energy in their work. To struggle to hear one's own voice rather than that imposed by critics or publishers of whatever Color is a difficult journey.

I often wish that I were a comedian or singer, that I could help an audience laugh and forget their personal sadness. At times we wish to escape from the steady, unrelenting confrontations. Just as all remedies are not soothing, many Chicana poets offer their listeners cures that sting.

Diagnosis

No llore, señora, no llore.
She whispers, "*No seré mujer,* doctor.

tears slide slowly down her cheeks
    as she pulls the white
        sheet against her skin

        No duele, señora, no duele.

wonders how to tell her man,
    "They will slit me
        open in a room of white
            lights, cut the dark
                warm place where our eleven
                    babies grew, throw the soft
                    bleeding part away."

        No llore, señora.

She fears her man
    will call her empty,
        fears he'll stop breathing
        hard when he hugs her
        late at night.

        No duele, señora.

She slides her finger where the scar
    will be, fears her laughter
        will now sink to that vacant space.

The doctor's blue eyes frown
at such a fuss over a useless uterus.[6]

Bitter. Unpleasant. Often writers from undervalued groups
seek this power, a mutual pain that can produce healing. The

poet offers the responsive listener respect—linguistic as well as cultural—sensitivity and understanding to internal conflicts, ties that bind. When cultural and linguistic barriers are removed, psychological needs can be met. Alienation and fear can be confronted. As a bilingual writer, then, I speak in English, the language in which I dream, the language with which I seek to order my world, but I incorporate the music and connotations of Spanish words and phrases. Listeners respond to the duality, I hope.

I must also be willing to display emotion to an audience comfortable with displays of feeling. I take the risk of establishing emotional bonds that ultimately is therapeutic as my generous listeners quickly and willingly share their stories of family ties, of painful discrimination. I confront my audience, knowing I must be listening to the tales of the past, to the cries and sighs of the present, and to the land: a bond we share.

At a time when indigenous health-care systems are being accorded more respect and viewed as legitimate health-care options, it would be encouraging if readings by non-Anglo writers were similarly viewed by those who profess belief in the power of the word. There is a mystery to language, for all the attempts to quantify and analyze it. Because no one group knows the secrets, hierarchies of worth should embarrass the perpetuator of that myth, who is often merely justifying his importance, as did physicians who frowned at herbal cures and traditional healers. We need more voices, and more varied voices, reading their stories and poems, reaching out to diverse audiences in complex and multiple ways. Our tongues must tell our stories. In that telling, we instruct and strengthen one another, the national community. If, like hands, words heal, soothe and calm or jolt and shock, that healing should be available to all. A woman with strong loyalties to an informal health system may feel alienated by an efficient but emotionally cold health clinic and be unable to relax and thus participate in the healing process. This same woman may attend a mainstream formal poetry reading or read a standard anthology and be alienated and isolated from the text. Her world is not being described or mentioned. She speaks the language, but little communication takes place. Certainly this was once the plight of female listeners and readers. The non-Western European voice is valid in its own key.

Writers of Color, Chicana writers, feel a moral responsibility to serve their own. Just as the *curandera* uses white magic, manipulates the symbols that are part of her patients' experience base to ease communication, the Chicana writer seeks to heal cultural wounds of historical neglect by providing opportunities to remember the past, to share and ease bitterness, to describe what has been viewed as unworthy of description, to cure by incantations and rhythms, by listening with her entire being and responding. She then gathers the tales and myths, weaves them together, and, if lucky, casts spells.

Notes

1. Pat Mora, *"Bruja:* Witch," in *Chants* (Houston: Arte Público Press, 1984), pp. 16–17.
2. Ruth Behar, "Sexual Witchcraft, Colonialism, and Women's Powers: Views from the Mexican Inquisition," in *Sexuality and Marriage in Colonial Latin America*, ed. Asunción Lavrin (Lincoln: University of Nebraska Press, 1989), p. 200.
3. Mora, "Curandera" in *Chants*, p. 26.
4. Mora, "Abuelita Magic," in *Chants*, p. 33.
5. Mora, "1910," in *Chants*, p. 31.
6. Mora, "Diagnosis," in *Borders* (Houston: Arte Público Press, 1986), p. 25.

Some words, some lines, some books get snagged in my head and linger. For years it has been the word *rearranged* brought to life in Mary Oliver's poem "Driving Through the Wind River Reservation: A Poem of Black Bear." For days after first reading this poem, I saw that black bear moving sluggishly as the earth warmed.

> . . . . In the distance
> the ice began to boom and wrinkle
> and a dampness
> that could not be defeated began
> to come from her, her breathing
> enlarged, oh, tender mountain, she rearranged
> herself so that the cubs
> could slide from her body, so that the rivers
> would flow.[1]

I felt—and feel—inside that bear's dark, thick fur, felt my body *rearranging*. What skill to heed the flickers and shimmers of our world with such care, to record nature with such reverence. What skill to set that word so carefully on the line. Mary

Oliver, whom I may never meet, was teaching me the craft of poetry. Such teachers are many. And for me, such teachers are often female, teachers attentive to our entanglements.

Most are poets, though I remember the freedom I felt when I saw Ntozake Shange's *for colored girls who have considered suicide / when the rainbow is enuf*, a work inviting me to dare such abandon. I remember wistfully when my days allowed more time with the works of Toni Morrison, Maxine Hong Kingston, Louise Erdrich, all describing strong women. Now I hand the books to my children. I remember the PBS special on Georgia O'Keeffe, stark as the Southwest landscape she loved. I still smile at her laughing confession that by painting huge flowers, she forced us to notice, much as the work of non-Anglo writers in this country says to us, "Notice."

We too seek to force a society to notice the bitter and the sweet. Often we both participate in our communities and are solitary writers, a tension. The mere cover of Denise Levertov's *The Poet in the World* reminds me of her firm conviction: "Both life and poetry fade, wilt, shrink when they are divorced."[2] Lorna Dee Cervantes, Sandra Cisneros, Alice Walker, Lucille Clifton, Amy Tan, Joy Harjo, and Linda Hogan are thick in the struggle of their people, and their writing is part of that struggle. Though the daily realities—high dropout rates, low per capita income, high unemployment—continue, these women teach me that the arrangement and rearrangement of work on the page is neither elitist nor irrelevant. It is the appropriate task of the person who weaves words for people's use. I seldom see *mis colegas Chicanas,* but they diminish my loneliness. Angela, Sandra, Ana, Denise, Vangie, Helena, Rosemary, Gloria, Erlinda, Demetria, Alicia, all struggle with me to write our stories and poems.

It is the poets to whom I return over and over. Their writing gives me hope. Women writers steadily feed me, as Rukeyser said they would. Not that the fare is all warm comfort. I re-read Lorna Dee Cervantes. "Every day I am deluged with re-minders / that this is not / my land / and this is my land."[3] A Sharon Olds poem makes me shut the book as the poem moves through me, poems such as "Young Mothers I" of deep, dark mother love,

> That look of attention
> on the face of the young mother
> like an animal
> bending over the carriage, looking up
> ears erect, eyes showing
> the whites all around.[4]

Olds states the private—thoughts, words, images—too raw to arrange and rearrange. But she does.

It was Margaret Atwood who fascinated me in about 1980. I found her in the unpopular poetry section at the university library. I was riveted by her hardness. "I approach this love / like a biologist / pulling on my rubber / gloves & white lab coat."[5] Over and over I returned to her books and finally sat down one day with lined paper and a number two pencil.

There is never enough time for the books I want to read. I try to first read what will tempt me to write. Every month or so I try to return to Lucille Clifton's words in "the making of poems":

> the reason why I do it
> though I fail and fail
> in the giving of true names
> is i am adam and his mother
> and these failures are my job.[6]

I journeyed to watch the weavers in Chiapas, to see their hands link generations through designs, to watch as they confronted their cloth, "white space," created their poetic designs. I longed to get tangled and snagged in their threads, then to break that spell my paper/pen way, sitting alone as my unseen teachers do, rearranging words on the page.

I reread Cisneros's *My Wicked Wicked Ways* and marvel line by line at the voice so clear and rhythmic. I hear her *abuelito,* "who used to laugh like the letter k."[7]

I met the Ohio poet David Citino for the first time recently. I carry his words with me. He said that he tries not to frighten beginning students when he speaks to them about the responsibilities of being a poet, that it has everything to do with their lives, that indeed we write struggling to learn how best to live our lives. Uruguayan writer Eduardo Galeano reminds us that *"we are what we do, especially what we do to change what we are:* our identity resides in action and in struggle."[8] I wonder how often such notions are discussed in writing classes and workshops. It is, of course, what Rilke was saying to us in *Letters to a Young Poet,* a book I read at least once a year. In his gentle way he guides us: "Being an artist means, not reckoning and counting, but ripening like the tree which does not force its sap and stands confident in the storms of spring without the fear that after them may come no summer."[9] For their music and images, I keep Lorca and Neruda close by. I am in awe of Galeano's moral fire as well as of Annie Dillard's intensity. Like many writers, I read books in which writers discuss their work habits and work. We are curious about why people like us do what they do. But the books I return to are those in which the author broods a bit, reminds me that there is no safe topic, message, form. Irish Poet Seamus Heaney speaks of creating a poem as "release." We earn the poem by following it rather than directing or leading it. "The tongue, governed for so long in the social sphere by considerations of tact and fidelity, by nice obeisances to one's origin within the minority or the majority, this tongue is suddenly ungoverned," writes Heaney.[10] It is frightening, of course, not to know where I am going in the mesh of words. On the other hand, a blank piece of paper is a way of giving myself space, to explore what will happen. Poetry is both an act of faith and an act of hope.

When Adrienne Rich accepted the National Book Award in 1974, she accepted it not only for herself, but also on behalf of the other two women nominated—Audre Lorde and Alice Walker. Rich stated, "We believe that we can enrich ourselves more in supporting and giving to each other than by competing against each other." The poets, writers, artists, who most deeply affect my work teach me not only about craft but also about values, harmony. The first time I met Denise Levertov, a poet whose humanity I had long admired, I was visiting Arturo Islas's class at Stanford. Denise did what I hope we can all do for one another. "My dear," she said, "if you're going to give a reading, you'll need water." She returned a few minutes later bearing a paper cup as I stood there mouth open. My unseen mentors teach me not only about rearranging words: they teach me about rearranging a life.

Notes

1. Mary Oliver, "Driving Through the Wind River Reservation: A Poem of Black Bear," in *Dream Work* (Boston: Atlantic Monthly Press, 1986), p. 31.

2. Denise Levertov, *The Poet in the World* (New York: New Directions Books, 1960), p. 112.

3. Lorna Dee Cervantes, "Poem for the Young White Man Who Asked Me How I, an Intelligent, Well-read Person Could Believe in the War Between Races," in *Emplumada* (Pittsburgh: University of Pittsburgh Press, 1981), pp. 35–37.

4. Sharon Olds, "Young Mothers I," in *Satan Says* (Pittsburgh: University of Pittsburgh Press, 1980), p. 40.

5. Margaret Atwood, "Their Attitudes Differ," in *Selected Poems* (New York: Simon and Schuster, 1976), p. 149.

6. Lucille Clifton, "the making of poems," in *two-headed woman* (Amherst: University of Massachusetts Press, 1980), p. 24.

7. Sandra Cisneros, "Abuelito Who," in *My Wicked Wicked Ways* (Bloomington, Ind.: Third Woman Press, 1987), p. 7.

8. Eduardo Galeano, "In Defense of the Word," in *Multi-cultural Literacy* (St. Paul: Graywolf Press, 1988), p. 121.

9. Rainer Maria Rilke, *Letters to a Young Poet* (New York: W. W. Norton, 1934), p. 30.

10. Seamus Heaney, *The Government of the Tongue: Selected Prose 1978–1987* (New York: Farrar, Straus, and Giroux, 1989), p. xxii.

17

TO GABRIELA,
A YOUNG WRITER

The enthusiasm and curiosity of young writers is source of energy. In one sense, we are all fledgling writers. With each new piece, we embark on the mysterious process again, unsure if we can describe or evoke what is in our minds and hearts. Sometimes it is difficult to convince those under thirty that the struggle never ends, that art is not about formulas. Maybe that continuing risk lures us. Luckily, octogenarians such as movie director Akira Kurosawa or Mexican painter Rufino Tamayo show us that we need never retire, and that what we have to share near the end of our lives may be far more lyrical than our early efforts in any art form. A sad truth about art is that it is unlinked to virtue. Wretches can write well while saints produce pedestrian passages.

I like to share what little I know, to encourage beginning writers. When a friend asked if I'd give her thirteen-year-old daughter some advice, I wrote her.

Dear Gabriela,

Your mother tells me that you have begun writing poems and that you wonder exactly how I do it. Do you perhaps wonder why I do it? Why would anyone sit alone and write when she could be talking to friends on the telephone, eating mint chocolate chip ice cream in front of the TV, or buying a new red sweater at the mall?

And, as you know, I like people. I like long, slow lunches with my friends. I like to dance. I'm no hermit, and I'm not shy. So why do I sit with my tablet and pen and mutter to myself?

There are many answers. I write because I'm a reader. I want to give to others what writers have given me, a chance to hear the voices of people I will never meet. Alone, in private. And even if I meet these authors, I wouldn't hear what I hear alone with the page, words carefully chosen, woven into a piece unlike any other, enjoyed by me in a way no other person will, in quite the same way, enjoy them. I suppose I'm saying that I love the privateness of writing and reading. It's delicious to curl into a book.

I write because I'm curious. I'm curious about me. Writing is a way of finding out how I feel about anything and everything. Now that I've left the desert where I grew up, for example, I'm discovering how it feels to walk on spongy fall leaves and to watch snow drifting *up* on a strong wind. I notice what's around me in a special way because I'm a writer, and then I talk to myself about it on paper. Writing is my way of saving my feelings.

I write because I believe that Mexican Americans need to take their rightful place in U.S. literature. We need to be published and to be studied in schools and colleges so that the stories and ideas of our people won't quietly disappear. Although I'm happy when I finish the draft of a poem or story, deep inside I always wish I wrote better, that I could bring more honor and attention to those like the *abuelitas,* grandmothers, I write about. That mix of sadness and pleasure occurs in life, doesn't it?

Although we don't discuss it often because it's depressing,

our people have been and sometimes still are viewed as inferior. Maybe you have already felt hurt when someone by a remark or odd look said to you: you're not like us, you're not one of us, speaking Spanish is odd, your family looks funny.

Some of us decide we don't want to be different. We don't want to be part of a group that is often described as poor and uneducated. I remember feeling that way at your age. I spoke Spanish at home to my grandmother and aunt, but I didn't always want my friends at school to know that I spoke Spanish. I didn't like myself for feeling that way. I sensed it was wrong, but I didn't know why. Now, I know.

I know that the society we live in and that the movies, television programs, and commercials we see all affect us. It's not easy to learn to judge others fairly, not because of the car they drive, the house they live in, the church they attend, the color of their skin, the language they speak at home. It takes courage to face the fact that we all have ten toes, get sleepy at night, get scared in the dark. Some families, some cities, some states, and even some countries foolishly convince themselves that they are better than others. And then they teach their children this ugly lie. It's like a weed with burrs and stickers that pricks people.

How are young women who are African American, Asian American, American Indian, Latinas, or members of all the other ethnic groups supposed to feel about themselves? Some are proud of their cultural roots. But commercials are also busy trying to convince us that our car, clothes, and maybe even our family are not good enough. It's so hard today to be your self, your many interesting selves, because billboards and magazines tell you that beautiful is being thin, maybe blonde, and rich, rich, rich. No wonder we don't always like ourselves when we look in the mirror.

There are no secrets to good writing. Read. Listen. Write. Read. Listen. Write. You learn to write well by reading wonderful writing and by letting those words and ideas become part of your blood and bones. But life is not all books. You become a better writer by listening—to your self and to all the colors, shapes, and sounds around you. Listen with all of your senses. Listen to wrinkles on your *tía*'s, your aunt's, face.

Writers write. They don't just talk about writing just as dancers don't just talk about dancing. They do it because they love it and because they want to get better and better. They practice and practice to loosen up just as you practiced and practiced when you were learning to talk. And because you practiced, you don't talk the way you did when you were three.

Do you know the quotation that says that learning to write is like learning to ice-skate? You must be willing to make a fool of yourself. Writers are willing to try what they can't do well so that one day they can write a strong poem or novel or children's book.

After a writer gains some confidence, she begins to spend more and more time revising, just as professional ice-skaters create and practice certain routines until they have developed their own, unique style. You probably don't like rewriting now. I didn't either until a few years ago.

How or why a book or poem starts varies. Sometimes I hear a story I want to save, sometimes it's a line, or an idea. It would be as if you saw someone dance and you noticed a step or some special moves and for a few days you didn't actually try the steps, but off and on you thought about them. Maybe you even feel the moves inside you. And then one day you just can't stand it anymore and you turn on the music and begin to experiment. You don't succeed right away, but you're having fun even while you're working to get the rhythm right. And slowly you loosen up, and pretty soon you forget about your feet and arms, and you and the music are just moving together. Then the next day you try it again, and maybe alter it slightly.

My pen is like that music. Usually I like to start in a sunny spot with a yellow, lined tablet and a pen. I have a number of false starts like you did dancing. I'm working but having fun. Alone. The first line of a poem is sometimes a hard one because I want it to be an interesting line. It may be the only line a reader will glance at to decide whether to read the whole piece. I'm searching for the right beginning. I play a little game with myself. (This game works with any kind of writing.) I tell myself to write any line no matter how bad or dull, because I can later throw it away. If I sit waiting for the perfect line, I might never write the poem. I'm willing to make a fool of myself. So I start, usually slowly. I write a few lines, read them aloud, and often start again. I keep sections I like and discard the uninteresting parts. The next day I read my work and try to improve it. I'm trying to pull out of myself the poem or story that's deep inside. It's important not to fall in love with the words you write. Pick your words or phrases, and then stand back and look at your work. Read it out loud.

You and I are lucky to be writers. So many women in history and even today who could be much better writers than I am have not had that private pleasure of creating with words. Maybe their families think writing is a waste of time, maybe they don't believe in themselves, maybe they have to work hard all day and then have to cook and clean and take care of their children at night, maybe they've never been taught to read and write.

I hope that you develop pride in being Mexican American and that you discover what you have to say that no one else can say. I hope that you continue writing, Gabriela.

EMERGING VOICES
The Teaching of Writing

Recently I've been reading the poet A. R. Ammons. In his poem "Corson's Inlet," he examines the natural world around him and reflects on his desire to allow himself "eddies of meaning" and further "no propaganda, no humbling of reality to precept." The poem ends, ". . . there is no finality of vision . . . tomorrow a new walk is a new walk."[1]

Ideally each of our serious conversations with one another is like a "new walk." What we bring is questions, ultimately, not answers. We search together, bringing our best selves to the task, knowing that today's conclusions will be but Ammons's "easy victories" if tomorrow we are unwilling again to walk and think anew.

The educational process is not only about knowledge. It is also a political and psychological process, notions that make us—or certainly me—uncomfortable. How calming it once was to believe in educational objectivity, that what was best and accurate and relevant appeared in textbooks, museums, documentaries. Ah, but textbooks, curricula, and policies are written by humans, those complex creatures who are shaped in part by their environment: their culture, family, religion, sex, language, economic status, nationality. We are all breathing bundles of prejudice: professors, curators, editors, filmmakers, writers. All of us. As Wendell Berry says, "We are humans—which means that we not only *have* problems but *are* problems."[2]

We know we are a marvel on the evolutionary chain precisely because we can communicate a rich and vast human inheritance to the next generation. We savor our means: language, art. We are readers and writers in part because we wish to participate in that process of gaining and sharing knowledge, insights. But has everyone been equally allowed to participate in that process? Should they be? Are all voices equal?

A Native American saying is, "Those who tell the stories rule the world." A cynic might today say that those who design our television commercials and videos rule the world to come, and indeed the impact of media cannot be underestimated; but readers know the power of language. Who writes and is published by major presses? Who writes our history and who selects what will be labeled our literature? Who proposes our metaphors?

In their interesting book *Metaphors We Live By*, George Lakoff and Mark Johnson state that metaphors are more than words. They are ways of perceiving reality. Words determine what we will notice and what we will ignore. Certainly the metaphor of this country as a melting pot is deep in our national psyche. We are a country of immigrants, but perhaps beginning with the nativist movement of the 1850s, we asked as psychological proof of citizenship a willingness to abandon ethnic culture and shed traditions. Yet hope arrives on our borders every day. Do we as a nation struggle to be worthy of that hope?

Though the melting-pot metaphor is outdated, movements like English Only attest to a national uneasiness about otherness, difference, diversity. A quick historical review of language policy will illustrate that these are more than educational issues.

They are political issues that often mask attitudes about a particular group, about acceptability, about linguistic choice.

Nervousness when confronted with otherness is natural. I'm sometimes surprised that we can't say that more easily. We know about fear of the unknown. We also know that power is pleasant. It is seldom relinquished willingly. But those darned demographers keep telling us that by the year 2000, one in three persons walking our streets will be of non-European ancestry. The face of U.S. North America is literally changing. Sometimes I feel that those of us who are labeled minorities, the global majority, are viewed as killer bees, wild hordes invading this country. For many of us, it is our country too. To whom a country belongs is an issue debated here, in South Africa, in Eastern Europe.

Dare we admit that there is and always will be bias in the educational process? Do we agree that the process should be not only intellectually challenging but also relevant and sensitive to our students? If so, how do we relate this belief to the teaching of writing?

On the one hand, we often tell beginning writing students to write what they know. We assign them primarily Western European literature and state that it reflects our national reality, that it can serve as a model. But when our students look into the literary mirror that we present, what do they see? Do they see themselves? Do they see people like themselves delving into their personal realities and shaping their frustrations, fears, dreams into moving literary works?

True, there are human universals that unite us, but there are also cultural values, traditions, and perspectives that are not universally shared. And what rich sources for writing such realities and their friction with the dominating culture can be if students perceive those topics as appropriate subject matter. I remember reading some of my *abuelita* poems to a class on women's literature some years ago. At the end of the class a young woman stated in some surprise, "Oh. I never thought about writing about my *abuelita*."

Like me, she probably had never been asked in her formal educational experience to read works by Latin American writers or by U.S. Latinos, a part of her literary heritage. How do we en *courage,* how do we nurture in young writers the courage to heed Pindar's directive, "Become what you are," as a writer boldly infuse your work with the rhythms, images, languages that you have inherited?

Perhaps as psychological proof of literary critical skills we have asked those of non-European backgrounds to equate one tradition with quality, to learn what the powerful Uruguayan writer Eduardo Galeano termed "the code of the initiated."[3] How receptive to other voices are we?

Not all ethnic groups in these United States are equally heard, not all of our voices are yet part of what is labeled American literature, using the label chauvinistically to mean approved literature in the United States. Some might say and do say that the worthy have been canonized. The issue, of course, is who determines worth. I smiled at Henry Louis Gates, Jr.'s sassy essay published in the *New York Times Book Review* that ends, "It was a tough job, being a canonical author. But somebody had to do it."[4]

The jazz wonder Miles Davis says, "I tell white players, 'Don't forget you're white. Play what you know.'" Wonderful irony. But it's hard to "play what you know" if you perceive that what you know is not valued by your society, by your professors.

I write for many reasons, among them pleasure and discovery. But I also write and am driven to write to "bear witness," to use James Baldwin's phrase. I'm not referring to polite nostalgia.

I write to record the stories of men and women still invisible in our literary landscape. Although I'm painfully aware of my linguistic failings, I still write. My work often requires confronting my readers with disturbing issues and images. But when a woman in Iowa whose parents were migrant workers comes up to me after a reading and says, "I've never heard a writer read about me before," you can be sure that sends me back to my desk in a hurry.

Writing is my means of working for my group, my attempt at creating something both beautiful and useful, my proper work in my community. But I use group and community in the broadest sense, for ultimately my community is not only my ethnic community but also all like-minded souls seeking a more equitable world. Another of Ammons's poems, "Poetics," ends with the fine notion that a poem summons "itself / through me / from the self not mine but ours,"[5] that wonderful, mysterious reality of our collective self.

Indeed it is much more difficult for us to evaluate writing and to guide beginning writers not only in terms of linguistic precision but also in terms of authenticity. How do we nudge them to release that inner voice, that private speech that is unique, that has life—both singular and shared?

We humans are a conundrum. The current global environmental movement illustrates our membership in a human community. We are like yet unlike. Odd that we are more dazzled by diversity in the wild—in rain forests and snow-crusted valleys—than by our own human diversity.

Not only do students need textbooks that present this country's, and the world's, varied voices, we all need books and anthologies in our classrooms and homes that increase the likelihood that emerging voices will challenge and comfort and disturb and surprise us. How do we create space for new voices and assist them to learn from the great Midwestern trees outside my window? How do we teach them "Tree-wisdom," to center and rise, how "A tree surprises itself, year after year, / climbs its rings, / climbs itself."[6]

Notes

1. A. R. Ammons, "Corson's Inlet," in *The Selected Poems* (New York: W. W. Norton, 1955), p. 46.

2. Wendell Berry, "People, Land, and Community," in *Multi-cultural Literacy*, ed. Rick Simonson and Scott Walker (St. Paul: Graywolf Press, 1988), p. 44.

3. Eduardo Galeano, In Defense of the Word," in *Multi-cultural Literacy*, p. 121.

4. Henry Louis Gates, Jr., "Canon Confidential: A Sam Slade Caper," *New York Times Book Review*, 25 March, 1990, p. 38.

5. Ammons, "Poetics," in *The Selected Poems*, p. 61.

6. Pat Mora, "Tree-Wisdom," *Communion* (Houston: Arte Público Press, 1991), p. 85.

UNIVERSITIES

A Mirage?

Writing is untidy and disconcerting. No successful ad company would want to market it. It's not fast, it's not predictable, it's not sweet. First we fantasize about that hushed moment when we'll be wonderfully alone with all our familiar, comforting writing implements at hand. I visualize a sunny room and my cup of tea. We savor the moment when, bulging with inspiration and wisdom, we at last lift our pen or start our computer and begin a new work. And work it is, though we forget that aspect in the amnesia necessary to bring us back to the blank page.

Initially, I experience a degree of personal frustration when I finally have the quiet I crave. I begin to ask myself how in a world so full of turmoil—abused children, earthquakes, street people, burning cities—how I can detach myself from so much human need. My hands feel heavy, useless. A more selfish internal voice also mutters in annoyance. It whines that the days are getting longer again and that what my old friend Winnie the Pooh called "a spring zephyr" beckons me out for a leisurely walk. Annoyed, I confront self-imposed isolation.

Reluctantly I begin to lift words and feel their weight, ponder their shape, attempt to visualize a new verbal design in which these words might fit. Again I experience frustration. Every age has its laments, and certainly one of ours is that once-sturdy words such as *leadership* and *vision* are limp from overuse. The careful writer knows that noble concepts soon smack of salesmanship if the labels are also used in trendy slogans for cars and cosmetics. Exorbitant sums are paid to those who can manipulate language to unleash the consumer lurking with dilated pupils in each of us. Billboards, television, and magazine ads bombard us not only with clever images but with clever phrases that desensitize us to heeding language with care.

Such frustrations are far easier to handle, however, than the doubt. Ideally we come to the blank page our bare selves, for in our lucid moments we sense that it is only our least public self who can significantly contribute to the human conversation. How naked we feel without our titles, degrees, awards, lists of publications; how inarticulate, uncreative, eminently unsuited to the task, lonely.

Minority writers perhaps feel a particular kind of discomfort, sensing that their words may either be subjected to particular scrutiny or scanned with indifference, that the many whom they are thought to represent deserve a more effective voice. We also worry about serving our community. Like English professor John Wideman, we wonder, "At what point do our words become an irrelevance to the people who nurtured us, whose lives we sought to touch and celebrate when we embarked on a quest for knowledge? . . . Mastering the master tongue remains a perilous enterprise for the minority writer."[1]

But experience teaches us to have faith in the writing process. Haltingly we begin, heeding all our selves rather than censoring our comments as we do daily. In the initial writing phase, we struggle to respect and value our internal voices, to be uncertain, critical of our usual stance, undogmatic.

Writers are motivated to endure and, in fact, to welcome this frustrating process because it leads to discoveries, a unique fulfillment. We are curious beings, and we're willing to suffer in order to observe what our mysterious minds and hearts can produce. And to be candid, once we begin to create a design, the play can be delightful. I'm far too cowardly to ski, but I would think my elation is akin to finally pushing off a steep slope. Attention and skill are required to avoid the humiliation of casts and crutches, but the exhilaration is grand. Of course, at each new section we trudge up heavy with ourselves.

Parenting is another of life's disconcerting processes. I'm referring not only to the terror of living with teenagers, those elusive beings who mysteriously possess the familiar bodies of our sweet, affectionate children, but also to the full realization that for all their bravado, our offspring are fragile. We can damage those we cherish most. But we ignore that awesome fact in our initial fantasies about parenting. We daydream about the soft, warm creature who will doze deliciously in our arms, about treating the world to a miniversion of ourselves, inquisitive, thoughtful, creative.

Like the solitary writer, we endure frustration. The tiny expected guest ignores clocks and our schedules, tugs us away from our professional commitments and deadlines. And worse: we have to confront the reality that a life is now in our inexperienced hands. How do we prepare them to avoid our mistakes? How do we protect them from the world's cruelty and danger? How do we nurture their talents? How do we guide them so that the world is indeed better for their presence in it?

Somehow, often through the faith of others in us, we begin to have faith in ourselves, faith in a parenting process that again requires that we struggle, flounder, scrutinize our motivations, heed our varied selves. It's also a process of discovery, of fulfillment, when approached with a necessary humility.

Is educating likewise a disconcerting process? Should it be? Should the responsibility for preparing world leaders and world citizens sober us? Though we may not dwell on it, we know that foreign heads of state as well as foreign cabinet members and business leaders are being trained at U.S. universities. Though we may not dwell on it, we know that in our technological era with its emphasis on degrees, most of our local, regional, and national leaders, whether in business, government, public service, education, or the arts, are being trained at our universities. Though we may not dwell on it, we know that given the power of U.S. electronic communications technology and the internationalization of U.S. business, students who learn at our institutions will one day make decisions with global implications.

Like writers and parents, members of the university community also enjoy their fantasies, educational fantasies, that is. After the grueling Ph.D. endurance test, faculty members long for quiet offices with their names on the door, for significant contributions to their discipline, for attentive—if not worshipful—students. Administrators fantasize too. Empty "in" boxes, a day with no committee meetings, completing a grant or report before the due date, time—to read, write a speech, design a new program.

The frustrations of university life are many: campus politics, scarce financial resources, professional jealousies. I wonder, however, whether we sufficiently acknowledge the frustration of clarifying and articulating our reason for existence.

And though it is very un-American to admit doubt, I believe we do feel a level of discomfort at daring to state why we exist. Deep inside we know that as soon as we exercise our right to clarify and define our mission, we will be asked to fulfill it. We practice avoidance. We expend our energies on specific departmental or programmatic issues, or—at our pettiest—on snickering at the incompetence of our colleagues.

When I had the privilege of visiting a rural development

project in the mountain region of the Dominican Republic, I learned about cold showers and the embarrassing arrogance of roosters. Jeep rides jostled my insides so, I wondered if my internal organs would ever find their way back to their original locations. But foreign travel is one of my great teachers. The visit allowed me not only to spend time with the historically poor and forgotten—children who trudge two hours to school with no breakfast, elderly men and women who weave thatch all day as their only means of support—but it also allowed me to witness a committed group of people who shared clear goals.

From the cooks to the director, each spoke passionately about why this project was important to the individuals served, to the region, to the future of the country. That vision was an obvious source of pure, concentrated energy. It allowed the group to prioritize, motivated the members to be inventive, to assess, to seek counsel. It pushed them out of themselves. The meals cooked, forests thinned, mininurseries started, fluoride lessons taught, funding sought—all were part of an inspiring whole. The vision was not hype; it was conviction.

We too need to become accustomed to articulating a shared vision among ourselves and with our society. Context is essential for discussing the different aspects of our role. Individual issues, be they academic freedom, student development, racial unrest, or research priorities, cannot be appropriately addressed until we agree on, or at least agree to continue discussing, the role of universities and then the role of our particular university.

Should the discussion be left to administrators? Should the steady clarification of an institution's mission be left to them? In an era of specialization, do faculty busy with grants, publishing, preparing their students to be competitive—do faculty have time for what some may view as esoteric discussions? I hope so. Surely a shared vision is a means of remaining engaged. Such a fine word, *engaged*. How can we motivate the next generation to set down their earphones and join the conversation if we too have removed ourselves by our frustration or apathy or cynicism?

Societies, citizens if you will, recognize that their intellectual inheritance as well as their present culture merits preserving and continued analysis, that inquiry can solve societal dilemmas, be they in health or economics. Scholarship, though perhaps not fully understood by all citizens, is deemed as a necessary and appropriate activity, as is teaching. Universities are also viewed as enhancing the life of the off-campus community, not only through sharing expertise and research knowledge but also through presenting artistic works that soothe or annoy or challenge us. I doubt that there would be much debate about these university roles: research, teaching, service.

And many would agree that the university should be *in* but not *of* the world, much as writers need to be and as families need to be in some ways islands or retreats. I do not by any means wish to imply vacation spots, beach-front property for the idle rich. Like wildlife sanctuaries, universities are spaces designated by society as vital for its own welfare and enhancement. In this case, space to insure society's intellectual life, a space a bit apart from the hustle-bustle of commerce, a space for study, reflection, creation. A space for searchers.

An inspiring notion, a community of searchers. What a privilege to be part of it. Costumes and masks required, of course, as in most human interactions. We're privileged, though, for a number of reasons. Not all who have the mental capacity to participate in the institutional dialogue have the opportunity to be part of the community of scholars. Economic and social class are often factors. Also, not to admit our privileged status would be insensitive. Hard as we may toil, we do not return at night to a scanty dinner with blistered feet and hands. And more, in a noisy world, we have the luxury of quiet, of books. Gleefully I say we have not only the opportunity but the obligation to read, to spend time with some of the most learned, inventive, wise, and disrespectful minds in human history.

If we are truly searchers, ours will be a steady process of questioning: questioning ourselves, one another, our department, college, university, society. Thus the university will exist in a state of tension both within itself and with its surroundings; a healthy and necessary tension, although in this age of diplomacy and consensus, such an attitude may be unappealing and unpopular. Just as individual faculty members question the tenets of their disciplines, push the boundaries of accepted theories, we need them to question the policies within the institution and participate in posing the university's questions to society. Just as we shape ourselves, we shape our institutions. Thus can the university truly lead, assist society to question itself.

Obviously a major societal institution is strongly influenced by external factors. In a media age, universities hire media experts to tell their stories; in an era of partnerships and economic emphasis, universities have more meetings with corporations and government agencies. But what questions do we pose, what limits do we set for those who wish to fund our research or conferences or endowments?

Money, money, money is incredibly seductive to institutions as well as to individuals. Although the acquisitive eighties are over, "want fever" remains highly contagious. Often we want in our university space what we want in our private lives. Like good capitalists we want new buildings, newer furniture and computers, bigger budgets, bigger salaries. Temptation glitters appealingly. How difficult to question the very entities whose financial support we need.

I am not referring to an arrogant questioning, a headline seeking, self-proclaimed keeper of morals who reminds us of the rooster crowing in self-absorption at daybreak in the Dominican Republic. I'm referring to an institutional stance based on the determination to steadily evaluate our decisions according to agreed-upon goals, to maintain integrity.

Too often the discussion about the role of the university ends with a sigh of relief at this point. Frustration and fear abate. We were on the right track after all. Add phrases like *strategic planning* and *enlightened self-interest* to the old mission statement, and we can end this time-consuming exercise and return to the concrete, to finishing a journal article, finalizing the budget, designing the fall schedule.

Can we believe that technological advances, dramatic demographic shifts, increased life expectancy, and expanded understanding of our global interconnectedness have no implications for the institutions that will educate many of this country's leaders? In commencement addresses, respected speakers eloquently challenge graduates to improve the world they have inherited. How often do we discuss this responsibility with first-year students, urging them and guiding them to wisely use their time on campus to prepare for the role society will have a right to expect? How often do we design educational experiences that indeed heighten a student's awareness of significant global issues: our threatened environment, economic disparity, bioethics, the world debt, imperiled cultures? How do we prepare responsible world citizens?

We will educate most of this country's bank and foundation executives, doctors, kindergarten teachers, physicists, city planners, newspaper editors, school board members, and presidents—as well as presidents of other countries. Don't we need to continue the discussion, to ask who will come to these privileged spaces as scholars and students, what contributions we and society have a right to expect as we preserve the past, propose solutions for the present, and prepare leaders and responsible citizens for the future?

Frustration. This may be more than we bargained for. We are experts in the discipline we wish to study and share. Careers and merit ratings nip at our heels. Well, if we're satisfied with the state of the world or too detached to risk involvement, we can return to our offices. Shut the door. Leave these awesome obligations to others. We can also confront a new, blank page with our fellow searchers, struggle and flounder as we trust the process, have faith in one another, listen to our varied selves, participate in the wearying but exhilarating process of change, of designing necessary educational institutions that have both intellectual and social responsibilities.

Even though bureaucracies are inherently sluggish, the role of the university is to be vital. Essential. Invigorating. The intellectual aspect of invigorating is clearly understood. Scholars and artists produce works that excite our individual and our collective imaginations. New theories about other galaxies and contemporary artistic expressions combining painting, film, light, and music—both tease our curiosity and heighten sensory perceptions. Our numbness is diminished when our fellow humans share their discoveries. We are more alive.

But our fellow humans are many and diverse. Should universities be attentive to the powerful and not the powerless? to the articulate and not the voiceless? to the aggressive and not the intimidated? At least in theory we reject the image of the ivory tower, are concerned about accountability. As privileged and moral women and men, aware of our comfortable, padded cocoon, can we dare to be complacent about existing human injustice?

Much in our society encourages us to avoid the painful. Solitude and silence are not in style. We can watch television while we eat, listen to music while we run, talk on the telephone while we drive. We can be busy and distracted, fill our minds with facts and figures. If we talk loud enough and long enough, we can forget those who daily endure oppressive regimes; we can forget Them. Them. The parents whose baby died of starvation this morning. Them. The children who started crying when armed soldiers grabbed their grandmother. Them. The writers who memorized their revolutionary poems in dark prisons last night. If *we* can forget them, our students can.

The questions we pose to society surely must include questions about the worth of the individual, about our shared humanity. Organizations such as Amnesty International nobly labor to insure that human rights violations will not go unnoticed. Penetrating our personal and institutional insulation is a huge challenge, however. We too often assume that being entertained is somehow our right. With the click of a remote-control switch we can avoid confronting the brutal, the tragic. Even when we plan to read serious news accounts, we can sink into our favorite newspaper or magazine in our temperature-controlled home and read somewhat comforting descriptions of nuclear arms de-escalation and progress in cancer research. At a deep level we know that injustice plagues the planet, that other men, women, and children are not free: not free to travel, not free to practice their religion, not free to speak their convictions without reprehensible reprisals. We know that today others who like us sing their babies to sleep, gasp at a falling star, shriek when a loud noise startles them from a deep sleep, that other humans breathe fear. Some are nervously whispering their opinions even as we walk across our calm campus, fiercely and loudly stating our beliefs.

When I visited Cuba, I saw much that impressed me—truly accessible health care for all, streets that were safe even late at night, artists engaged in both their work and their world—but I thought a lot about my tongue while I was there, about free speech. As I walked the beaches alone, as I listened to the revolutionary fervor of our guides, I thought about how intolerable it would be for me to raise my three hyper-talkative, hyper-critical children in an atmosphere of verbal restraint. I thought about risk and oppression. I thought about the painful risk for conscientious parents in violently repressive societies who raise their children to think critically and yet know that those very thoughts and words may bring them harm. I thought about the parental temptation to cover their mouths, to stifle their fiery, combustible questions. Never before had I fully valued free speech, felt the combined intellectual and physical pleasure of opening my mouth and stating or shouting what I felt in my bones. I realized on that beautiful island of Cuba what an important legacy we have to leave our children, a legacy we must cherish and protect. As you can sense, it is in my trips out of this country that I best see our weaknesses and our strengths.

The sixties will be remembered as a time when fists clenched at societal injustices. Today, sadly, the fist often clenches wadded dollar bills; issues of oppression merit little attention from the pragmatic seduced by the glitzy life: fast cars, fat wallets. What role do we play in expanding students' awareness, in assisting them to analyze conflicting forces, power struggles, whether international or local?

If we have accepted tension rather than complacency as our lot, then in this space for study, reflection, and creation we need, and students need, to hear society's turmoils: white pride, gay rights, ethnic pride, pro-life, drug testing, voluntary segregation, freedom of the press, apartheid, AIDS advocacy. Few if any of us would disagree that part of the campus experience should include the opportunity to listen to society's unresolved issues. Most, if not all, will be disconcerting. Memories of the sixties may alarm those who, like our politicians, would focus our attention only on the positive.

Simply disseminating rules for rallies and demonstrations is to ignore our institutional obligations. Aware that as a country we value the slick, aggressive, precise, wealthy, white, how do we create occasions for the historically marginalized to be heard? We can begin by confronting our personal and institutional stereotypes and demonstrate to students by our actions and policies, including curriculum reform, the process of steadily evaluating myths, symbols, values, assumptions, and priorities. Such moral leadership requires considerable courage, but then so does using the label *university*.

There is unrest on many campuses not unlike the unrest in our cities. And although certain human rights are protected in this country, oppression exists. The economic and educational underclass continues to grow. More and more we are a divided society. We hide in our safe neighborhoods. How do universities address the national social ills of homelessness, rising health-care costs, environmental degradation, drugs, dropouts, and discrimination?

Presidential campaigns include lengthy descriptions by both parties of the promise of democracy, of our national struggles and our national triumphs. Fortunately, references to this country as a "melting pot" are disappearing as we become more aware of the value of cultural and ethnic diversity, although movements such as English Only reveal a national discomfort with our changing demographics. These United States *are* changing, as they have changed from their beginnings. And if universities are to fulfill their intellectual and social responsibilities, they too must continue their disconcerting struggle to remain vital to their country, vital to its diverse citizens.

Many of these citizens are immigrants, who like their predecessors came to this country seeking a better life for their children. The hopes of these immigrants maintain what is perhaps our country's oldest tradition. Their fears deserve our attention.

wrap their babies in the American flag,
feed them mashed hot dogs and apple pie,
name them Bill and Daisy,
buy them blonde dolls that blink blue
eyes or a football and tiny cleats
before the baby can even walk,
speak to them in thick English
        hallo, babee, hallo
whisper in Spanish or Polish
when the babies sleep, whisper
in a dark parent bed, that dark
parent fear, "Will they like
our boy, our girl, our fine american
boy, our fine american girl?"[2]

Change produces tension. We are all bundles of prejudice. Alone in the dark we know this. Sadly, as Chicana critic Gloria Anzaldúa reminds us, racism is "cultivated and produced in families, churches, temples and state institutions."[3] Cultivated. Think of the horror of it. Humans continue to expend their needed energy and creativity in planting tiny, hard seeds of hate in soil part pride, part fear. We nurture the tender vines and their tiny thorns that spread like evil whispers in the dark. Confronting Otherness, then, can be as uncomfortable as confronting silence or a blank page or parenthood. Understandably, we seek the known, the predictable. Communication advances, changing demographics, federal legislation prohibiting discrimination, all force us to tolerate the Other, who may not look like us, sound like us, agree with our values, match our image of what an "American" is. Sometimes we retreat to our homes, display our discomfort or fear or frustration at our loss of power and prestige by ethnic slurs and ethnic jokes. Sadly this even happens in university classrooms. What are advertisers teaching about cultural diversity when they appropriate cultural symbols to sell a product? What are we teaching the next generation about human rights? Why aren't we more offended by heavy-handed cultural domination in our own cities? Why are we surprised at racial eruptions in our cities and on college campuses if we are in fact ignoring predictable tensions?

We know that our perceptions of time, space, aesthetics, and, yes, quality are culture bound. "We are culturally constituted in complex ways and not just engendered in a homogenous situation," says critic Norma Alarcón.[4] How do we ensure that those teaching and those learning at our institutions reflect our national pluralism? To bristle at that question, to assume that equity dilutes quality, is racism.

In a college or university community struggling to discover new solutions, to reassess existing theories, we must welcome varied strengths and perspectives. We need them. Ours is not a closed club. Not sex nor age nor race nor physique determine the ability to think critically. Let's leave the body fetish to advertisers.

To be representative, universities need to recruit and retain more women and more scholars and students of non-European backgrounds. This democratization of higher education is inextricably tied to the social obligation of universities, specifically, to upholding the right in this country to pursue education regardless of one's background. The scholarly privilege cannot be tied to skin color. The contributions of non-Anglo scholars to their disciplines as well as their role in documenting and validating cultural identity, values, and history help counter a pernicious provincialism.

How can we teach our students a process of questioning,

urging them to glean insights and solutions from the breadth of human experience without embarking on this process ourselves? We can continue to define the world and human achievements in narrow terms—historically these were often white male achievements, often emphasizing the United States and Western Europe—or we can expand our curriculum and scholarship as well as determinedly seek scholars with varied perspectives. Can we put a finger on our tiny spot of the world and with total certainty proclaim its singular significance without feeling a bit like those roosters, a bit embarrassed at our arrogance? Discussions of what constitutes our most important literary heritage, for example, are necessary and valuable. The basic issue in such discussions, however, is not curriculum reform. The first question is: Do universities and their graduates have responsibilities to their societies, and if so, what are those responsibilities? Then we can address specific issues. The solutions will never be easy; the discussions never final.

As a writer, I would be remiss if I did not also mention what Eric Wolf states in his complex book *Europe and the People Without History*: "The ability to bestow meanings—to 'name' things, acts, and ideas—is a source of power. Control of communication allows the managers of ideology to lay down the categories through which reality is perceived."[5] Certainly the common use of the terms *developed* and *undeveloped* in reference to nations, of the terms *First* and *Third* World illustrate the power of labeling, the power to assign value. Do the children in our inner cities live in the "First World"? By omitting the adjective *technologically* before the word *developed*, we equate one of our present idols with the far more encompassing concept of human development. Technology is a means, not an end, and not always the best solution. Those who work in community development around the world and who value the wisdom of indigenous knowledge, for example, remind us that inappropriate technology, a huge tractor on a small Peruvian plot, can actually be counter to the economic development of a region.

Scholars know the power of naming as they define history, relevance. We are quick to accuse the media of agenda setting, of selecting the issues for public discussion through the power to focus our attention. Don't we through our publications also have a unique kind of power, might we even have been a bit seduced by that power when we chose this profession, and can we then in subtle ways deny that power to those not traditionally a part of the academy?

Once the expectation was that universities would educate a certain predictable portion of the young population. More and more the question is: In a democracy, who has the right to come to this space? Morally and pragmatically, should a university education be simply a system of inheritance? What responsibilities do universities have to the historically underrepresented? Is it enough to express regret at previous discriminatory admission practices?

Although the statement that all citizens deserve equal access seems a simple one, we know it is fraught with complications. Aware of the issue of test bias, universities continue to compete fiercely for the best test takers. Special mailings and phone campaigns aim to lure these multiple-choice experts and their number two pencils to our doors.

A main issue may be that we're not convinced that students from the emerging majority really belong on our campuses. Edward Hall in his book on nonverbal communication, *The Silent Language*, astutely observed that our behavior can imply that we view foreigners as "underdeveloped Americans."[6] Do we often view minority students in the same way, anxious to alter them, to help them assimilate, to help them become like us? I firmly believe that the question is not really how to recruit and retain minority students. We know about early intervention programs, support services, role models, mentoring, curriculum reform. The question is, Why should we recruit and retain them? Once we can—and do—articulate that response, jointly accept our responsibility rather than merely assigning it to a few non-Anglo staff members, then each institution can scrutinize its present systems, plan its strategies and assessment procedures.

Isn't ours a democracy, the belief in government by the people, by the citizens? Shouldn't all of our citizens, then, be welcome at our educational institutions at all levels, not only for economic reasons but also because of our national ideals? Admittedly, it's hard even to talk about our aspirations when we cringe at our political campaigns. As we witness current international courage in pursuit of governance by the people, though, surely the world's purported democratic leader had best do more than talk about ideals.

Money is, of course, an effective lure, tempting some universities to target minority students for that less-than-inspiring motive: enlightened self-interest. "Economic necessity has been added to the moral imperative heretofore expressed as the overriding reason for promoting diversity," says Manuel Pacheco, president of the University of Arizona.[7] Not surprisingly, economics and fear of litigation prompt change in ways issues of morality and justice seldom do. We hear about the challenge of remaining economically competitive in the international marketplace, for one of our current metaphors is that the country is, or should be, a competitive corporation. Our national educational goals often refer to inculcating in students virtues valued by business, such as loyalty and punctuality. We also hear that minorities are younger than the aging majority population. Recruiting minority students can help maintain enrollments in addition to easing our fretting about our threatened social security system. Dropouts are ultimately expensive to society, credit-hour production is a priority, as is a trained population to support us in our golden retirement years; therefore, let's educate minorities. The old bottom line rises off the page and spooks us again.

Some Anglo educators, sadly, still view their Central American, Cuban, Puerto Rican, or Chicano students as problems. The remark Mexico's most respected living woman writer, Elena Poniatowska, credits to writer José Augustín probably expresses the feeling of many bright Latino students. If they are dark skinned, they may too often be viewed at their schools and universities as "a shoe-shine boy made good."[8]

The role of universities in ensuring true access for academically talented students will require innovation and evaluation. Considering that educational preparation is unequal, how can we assist students with potential who have few if any guides through the preparation and application maze? Sadly some school counselors continue to track students based on ethnicity and class. How do we collectively create systems for attracting all students early in their educational experiences to view university education as a reasonable option if they prepare, plan, persist? How do we work with minority parents who far from being indifferent to their children's future are intimidated by institutions they do not understand? How do we dignify the nontraditional? What is our responsibility to parents like Elena?

My Spanish isn't enough.
I remember how I'd smile
listening to my little ones,
understanding every word they'd say,
their jokes, their songs, their plots.
Vamos a pedirle dulces a mama. Vamos.
But that was in Mexico.

Now my children go to American high schools.
They speak English. At night they sit around
the kitchen table, laugh with one another.
I stand by the stove and feel dumb, alone.
I bought a book to learn English.
My husband frowned, drank more beer.
My oldest said, "*Mamá,* he doesn't want you
to be smarter than he is." I'm forty,
embarrassed at mispronouncing words,
embarrassed at the laughter of my children,
the grocer, the mailman. Sometimes I take
my English book and lock myself in the bathroom,
say the thick words softly,
for if I stop trying, I will be deaf
when my children need my help.[9]

Given all the talent and creativity on university campuses, I have no doubt that effective programs to recruit and retain minority students can be developed. Not all faculty and staff will choose to participate, but such work should be evaluated and rewarded and should evolve from true institutional accountability. Some might contend that it is not part of a university's mission to invest institutional energies and resources to counter oppression. But can we settle for being enclaves of the advantaged? A true commitment to protecting civic rights requires that we struggle against injustice. Often on a university campus the struggle is in the form of rigorous analysis. The opportunity for that educational experience must exist for all.

Perhaps there is a certain irony in just how essential universities have become. Unfortunately our ideas and our questions may not always be viewed as necessary by the country, but our degrees certainly are. Most who wish to actively participate in the economic and civic life of our nation will come to us for training. And this whole notion of training is persistently and appropriately questioned, because a university education should be more than mere memorization and the development of marketable skills, more than a glorified high school experience. Surely a university experience should be disconcerting, as students struggle and flounder to understand their intellectual inheritance as well as the national and global issues that merit their attention and energies, as they struggle and flounder to articulate and justify their beliefs.

On that trip to the Dominican Republic, I was annoyed by a woman who persistently chided my country for not setting a good example. "You're powerful and wealthy," she would say heatedly. "It is your responsibility to lead." At each such interchange, I felt like a porcupine with my quills aquiver. "Don't wait for us," I'd counter. "We're busy watching the Super Bowl and MTV. We ignore our own homeless and hungry. To us you are part of our Caribbean playground."

I was frustrated by her demand and by my cold reply. I still see her fist clenched in determination. And her anguish was justified. As I experienced daily power failures and witnessed the struggles of her colleagues to serve isolated, forgotten communities, how could I deny our abundance, and how could I deny our responsibility?

How can *we* deny our responsibility, we, the universities in these United States, which in this technological era will graduate many of the country's future leaders? We and they are members of a society that not only tolerates but encourages voyeurism and consumerism. And given the clever marketing of these assorted seductions, little wonder that we either succumb or in disgust retreat to our offices and shut the door. But morally we cannot exist in isolation, for ourselves. To talk only to each other might smack of delusions of royalty, intellectual royalty, of course. This is not to imply that university faculty should become social workers, but neither are any of us, nor our institutions, freed of civic obligation.

Universities exist *in* society, and we fail if those societies are not improved by our presence and by the presence of our graduates. Universities have unique missions and unique personnel. Even when we work closely with our nonuniversity colleagues on issues such as economic development and environmental research, our role is not merely to mirror society, nor to accept its values. Although remaining intellectually independent while economically dependent is a significant challenge, a university can do no less.

Gabriel García Márquez says that the "writer's duty—his revolutionary duty, if you like—is to write well." Like many Latin American writers, I believe that the writer also has a responsibility to struggle against injustice in this unjust world. How individual writers labor against oppression is a decision for their conscience. Certainly it need not be by writing politically. Ethical answers elude automatic responses.

I have similar beliefs about universities. I believe they have social as well as intellectual roles, and that these responsibilities include demonstrating to society the role of the moral mind in identifying, analyzing, and participating in addressing contemporary issues. These imperatives also include demonstrating to society that a mind should not be judged by the shell that houses it, that all our funny-looking shells merit equal respect. Rather than continuing debates based on the false polarity of excellence or diversity, we can realize the truth in the perspective of University of California–Berkeley Chancellor Chang Lin Tien of "excellence through diversity."

When we engage in heated discussions about the nature of the university, we can savor the fire. Ideally we can return to our classrooms and offices with a heavier sense of personal obligation, with a willingness and determination to actively participate in shaping our institutions. Ideally we return willing to search collectively for methods to prepare citizens and leaders more aware of global and national problems, more determined to participate in solving them. Like the solitary writer and the conscientious parent, we will need to struggle, flounder, scrutinize our motivations, heed our varied selves.

I've spent most of my life on the U.S.-Mexican border. Daily I looked across the Rio Grande and saw the purple, pink, and turquoise homes of families with no running water. Some say that when those Mexican families look across that river, the buildings on the U.S. side look like a mirage. Throughout this world, women and men, our equals, view universities, our place of work and our role in them, as illusory. They shake their heads at our amazing good fortune.

Notes

1. John Wideman, in review of *The Signifying Monkey* by Henry Louis Gates, Jr. in *New York Times Book Review*, 14 August 1988, p. 3.
2. Pat Mora, "Immigrants," in *Borders* (Houston: Arte Público Press, 1986), p. 15.
3. Gloria Anzaldúa, "*Haciendo caras, una entrada*," in *Making Face, Making Soul: Haciendo Caras*, ed. Gloria Anzaldúa (San Francisco: Aunt Lute Foundation, 1990), p. xix.
4. Norma Alarcón, "The Theoretical Subject(s) of This Bridge Called My Back and Anglo-American Feminism," in *Making Face, Making Soul*, p. 364.
5. Eric R. Wolf, *Europe and the People Without History* (Berkeley and Los Angeles: University of California Press, 1982), p. 388.
6. Edward Hall, *The Silent Language* (Garden City, New York: Anchor Press, Doubleday, 1973), p. 24.
7. Manuel T. Pacheco, "Leadership in Higher Education: How It Manifests Itself" (Paper presented at symposium, "The Role of Higher Education and Latinos: Empowerment Strategies for the 1990s," University of Texas at El Paso, 6 February 1991), p. 4.

8. Elena Poniatowska, "A Question Mark Engraved on My Eyelids," in *The Writer on Her Work: New Essays in New Territory*, ed. Janet Sternberg (New York: W. W. Norton, 1991), p. 95.

9. Pat Mora, "Elena," in *Chants* (Houston: Arte Público Press, 1984), p. 50.

20

A POET FOR PRESIDENT

If the title made you flinch or smile, my suspicions are confirmed. Writers, and particularly poets, are viewed with skepticism in this country. We're considered mathematically unfit and organizationally inept, totally inappropriate candidates for what society calls "positions of responsibility." Also, you might be thinking, we dress funny.

Whether the topic is the presidency of the nation, a corporation, or an organization, many doubt that a serious writer is suitable to propose direction. Many U.S. writers may also doubt the wisdom of attempting these dual roles. In Latin America, on the other hand, those privileged with an education often serve in a variety of capacities. Writers are administrators, ambassadors, even aspire to be presidents of their countries. This reality is not part of our experience, of our separation of the arts from the state. Imagine the reaction if a poet announced that she is running for president or if a governor stated that he is a novelist. The arts and bureaucracy are viewed as antithetical. There is an unstated belief that writers should be a bit removed from the dailiness, the drudgery of this world. They can teach, farm, maybe serve as arts administrators—maybe. Politically correct (PC) occupations. The occasional poet/doctor or poet/executive is the exception. Often that other occupation is ignored as almost an embarrassment when the writer is discussed. Such narrow boxes we design for one another.

The economic, educational, and moral factors that motivate Latin American writers to participate in the more public life of their countries likewise exist in this country for Latina writers. Usually we have families to support, whether our children or our parents. We feel a responsibility in some way to motivate the next generation to resist the lure of material goods and to pursue their education, to invest in themselves. And we feel an urgency to speak out, to name, to insist that our community be heard locally, nationally, and internationally. Retreating from the world feels irresponsible.

Writing or speaking about that world, about migrant workers or public housing, may quickly be used in literary or university circles to prove that a Latina writer is not about art. It was Neruda who said, "In my poems I could not shut my door to the street."[1] The artistically pure of heart in this country write about wooing stubborn women but not about women struggling to learn English. Do artists have to make a choice? Can those determined to devote much of their time to their art also choose to be engaged in education reform or international development or environmental planning? Should the arts be a more important part of our national life?

Until about ten years ago, most of my energy was spent teaching and raising my three children, both rewarding and exhausting pursuits. I became a university administrator shortly after I had decided to devote more and more time to my writing. My fellow administrators endured but did not understand my determination to write. They wondered why, if I insisted on this compulsion, I didn't tackle substance: grants, reports, strategic plans. Some wished for this change because they were genuinely concerned about my professional career. An uncynical description of administrators would probably include words like *measured* and *organized,* hardly words we associate with writers. But I was persistent, particularly after my first poem was published in 1981. Like Kafka, I hung onto my desk with my teeth. Evenings and weekends, after dishes were washed and homework questions answered, I wrote.

Whereas my administrative friends tried discreetly to ignore my vice, the few writers I knew were suspicious of my daytime work. Some of us seem to have a knack for living in *nepantla,* that land in the middle, whether we want to or not. I was tainted by consorting with the manipulative. Although I'm suspicious of right and left brain dichotomies, certainly I know that different aspects of myself surfaced for each task, but I refuse to accept the notion that to maintain a certain credibility, the writer should absent herself from offices and leadership or from any activity that allows her to contribute. I tell beginning writers that there is no required uniform for being a writer. The image of the poet as the insufferable, arrogant male professor who can outdrink and outcurse all students or as the tortured loner wearing a black turtleneck and brooding on windy streets does little to encourage the young to discover through writing. Serious writing is not a shtick. It's work.

If writing made me a better administrator, and it did, why wouldn't I hope that among those motivated to raise their voices and perhaps seek and accept titles of responsibility would be men and women who also need time alone to think and create, whether with words or paint or music? Writing helped me to listen, which is the kind of administrative work that interested me, listening to the previously ignored and nudging and pressuring an institution or organization to do the same.

I did not enjoy the steady "push and pound, push and pound / 'Why am I the only Mexican American here?' "[2] But I did enjoy those years of being an advocate for my community, helping

Mexican Americans feel welcome, by their presence claiming what was their right, a presence and voice on their university campus. My favorite administrative position was that of campus museum director, because the role provided the greatest opportunity for play at work. I particularly enjoyed learning from my university colleagues across the Rio Grande. Those Mexican women did their administrative work with such human warmth and with such commitment to students. I often notice this firm sense of mission when dealing with Latin American educators. These are not dispassionate faculty members and administrators watching to see if the students can take the academic heat. They are teachers determined to help the next generation understand how essential—and exciting—learning can be. Rather than being detached observers, they are *in* the process with the students. The economic realities of their countries inspire them to engage the energies of the young.

These women from Juárez understood my need to work and to write. I benefitted from the concern I felt and feel about me as a person, a concern that can be so lacking on our rushed, rushed campuses. I benefitted because my Mexican counterparts were so willing to bring their expertise, talents, perspectives to the museum I directed. Often we U.S. citizens are much better at exporting our knowledge (and values) than at learning from others. International collaborative projects can often mean we're saying: let us show you how to do this right.

One of my clearest memories is of a museum opening on November second. Aware that *El Día de los Muertos,* the observance of Day of the Dead, is one of the more difficult traditions for Anglo-Americans to understand, and that many Mexican Americans do not fully understand this custom, we asked our colleagues in Juárez to help us. The traditional altars built on the museum lawn by Mexican students and teachers allowed us to see and briefly to experience the Mexican attitude toward death, that blend of sadness and humor, that penchant for joking about death that so shocks those raised with the notion that death constitutes the unspeakable. We saw candles, sugar skulls, fruit, Mexican sweet bread, old photographs, marigolds everywhere. We laughed together as we ate bread in the shape of skulls. Not a common evening pastime in the United States. But then we lived on the border.

The right to our cultural heritage has been the link between my administrative and writing work. Our ethnic legacy is our sixth sense, which assists us to understand our community, its history and values. I derived and derive particular pleasure from encouraging cultural exchanges. Why are they important? Why are they enjoyable yet not merely enjoyment, not merely occasions for relaxed conversation and laughter, important as those ingredients are in any human interchange? Our cultural differences are glorious. Like the proverbial fish unable to see the water in which it swims, we too can be blissfully unaware that our cultural inheritance shapes our values, perceptions, and reactions. Music, poetry, dance, let me feel, however briefly, a different rhythm, and in that rhythm I know what can elude logic. Such events instruct, humanize, and alert us to another value system that although neither better nor worse than our own, can provide new options for us, our human legacy.

Although we don't often admit it out loud, we know that our theories—even our scientific theories—reflect their era. The questions asked, the methodology, the funding priorities indicate the cultural and social issues of the day. Culture in its broadest sense, in its nonstatic sense, is not a marginal or inconsequential aspect of international collaboration. Our culture shapes us in ways we never see; it is as inseparable from us as our skin. It is not only language that may require translation, but also our behaviors and motivations.

I feel fortunate to have assisted international projects, to have learned about the exciting and depressing aspects of university administration, to have had occasions to speak about education and thus to think about the topic, just as I feel fortunate to have taught and to have raised my children. Because my society sees these various aspects of my life as competing rather than a complementary, I often do too. Candidly, I'm not sure that my years as an administrator improved my writing. Administration can encourage excessive caution and an oily language that lulls the reader or listener, dangerous habits. Because I distrust hierarchies, I feared, and may always be apprehensive about, combining administrative work with my writing. Would my head be so full of projects and details that I wouldn't hear the voices I wanted to hear? Would the pace in a society bent on increasing the work week and more supportive of planners than playwrights gobble my meager writing time, the time to do what I found most valuable, what was viewed as peripheral by my colleagues? At times administration was like a dark shark feeding on me.

How do I learn to resist the roles others create for me? As I tried to create time for each part of me, I envied males with a clear professional goal and with families ready to be supportive and understanding. Choosing to be a writer felt and can still feel like yet another way of marginalizing myself. Time was, and is, probably the greatest source of tension. I left administration in order to devote more of myself to my writing, to push myself as writer, to have more time to think about this world and us, the humans who fascinate me. I can't resist eavesdropping, anywhere. Politeness and the nudgings of my family prevent me from eavesdropping and staring too openly, from watching men, women, and children reach out from themselves and then pull back into themselves, we vulnerable creatures held together by a layer of thin skin.

Ultimately I bring more questions than answers. Like the

Mexican writer Elena Poniatowska, "I believe I will die like this, still searching, with a question mark engraved on my eyelids."[3] How do we resist our grand seducers: materialism, comfort, safety, apathy, laziness? How do we become more perceptive and help others to become more perceptive about our legacy of racism, about hierarchies of color, class, language? How do we become as excited about human diversity as we are about biological diversity in general? How do we learn to value ethnic heritage in a society that holds difference in low esteem? How do we develop the courage to live attentively, to heed the land, each other, ourselves?

When playwright Vaclav Havel, the president of Czechoslovakia, spoke before the Congress of the United States, he said that democracy will be an ideal as long as people are people. I often say Antonio Gramsci's words to myself, "pessimism of the intellect, optimism of the will."

Many artists may conclude that their work for their communities—broadly or narrowly defined—is their creative work, their poems or sculptures or symphonies. They view their responsible role as maintaining the distance required to do their work, to share what they bring forth from their bones. Artists bring that mysterious process to the communal table, the beauty and rage and hope and doubt. Neruda wrote that *"the writer's task has nothing to do with mystery or magic, and that the poet's, at least, must be a personal effort for the benefit of all. The closest thing to poetry is a loaf of bread or a ceramic dish or a piece of wood lovingly carved."*[4] Artists may justly fear the hypnotism of power, the distractions of visibility. Conspiring for the time necessary to exceed their perceived limits with sounds or bronze may mean that they must save themselves for this alone, forcing themselves to focus, saying no, no, no to most knocks at the door.

Disappointing others is not easy for women: we are conditioned to please. I can endure this guilt because I feel such frustration that year after year Latinas are ignored, that we are goaded to justify any place set aside for us just as we were once goaded to endure the places that weren't. Week after week I hear the voices of those annoyed at being asked to redefine the term *educated* in our society. Arrogantly they proclaim that *they* know what needs to be known. Their verbal swords gleam, polished with smooth, erudite allusions and with the spit of their perfected wit. They are ready to duel. I sigh, return to my new work, unwilling to expend my limited energy on the righteous, convinced that there are many words that demand our more careful use, including the word *American*. My fellow Americans live from Nome to Tierra del Fuego. I want to hear their oral traditions and to read their literature. In the fullest sense, I want to know and savor *American literature,* the literature of this continent and its peoples.

Where are the good-hearted souls struggling to prepare students to think critically in our changing, volatile society, to question our national arrogance and myths, to understand those around them? All the clever arguments will not change the fact: a multicultural society deserves a multicultural education.

Neither millionaires nor poets should be obvious choices for ethically guiding this nation or its institutions or communities. Each of us, regardless of daily work, is shaping this country, a country in need of our commitment and honor. We have a long way to go. More of us, dissatisfied with what we see and hear around us, dissatisfied with separatist solutions to complex problems, can create a community of conscience unwilling to be daunted by the enormity of our task. By not marginalizing the arts, by asserting that they are a valued and natural part of the country's life, we also encourage those who wish to pursue music or writing as a pastime to state this without feeling they are confessing a perversion. It is unwise for a society to view its artists as unfit for leadership, and it is unwise for artists themselves to believe that they are exempt from societal responsibilities. The issue, as with all stereotyping, is ensuring choice, aware that choice is a blessing of the privileged. Any individual wishing to actively and visibly serve society needs to have that option, whether she is tall or short, thin or fat, young or old, pale or dark, disabled or temporarily able-bodied, a bridge builder or writer. Some artists struggle against the world's inequities by pursuing their craft while holding an appointed or elected position or publicly advocating a cause. Others recoil at the tangle of such engagements, needing space and solitude. Complex issues of conscience, but society needs the involvement and voices of all.

How do we remember that we—humans—are the most vital natural resource on the planet, that we are ʳ ˡrces and reservoirs of energy? How do we exceed our self-perceptions and the assumptions of others and make our unique contribution?

Often when I read the newspaper or listen to the news, I wonder if my work has been irrelevant. I see refugees burying babies, overcrowded prisons, brutality sold as entertainment, this country dividing into the protected and the endangered. How does spending hours alone with my computer improve this world? And why do I face all the rejection slips, the loss of time with those I love, my solitary choice? I believe in the power of the word, that language shapes as well as reflects reality, that it creates space for difference, that our varied national voices strengthen us, not only in English but in all the rich languages that are part of these United States.

Recently, a Spanish-speaking gentleman, a rarity in Cincinnati, shook my hand and bowed slightly when he heard me say that I was a writer. I was surprised by his courtesy and congratulations, certainly not a common response to what I do. He went on to say, "I'm an artist too. I build bridges. And that is also an art, right?" Our society might do well to adopt that attitude, a more egalitarian attitude toward creativity that in no way diminishes what are called the *arts*, but that by removing them from a pedestal, makes them more a part of the country's life, a country in need of its artists' energy, intuition, and creativity. The vast capacity of the human spirit merits voices that assist us to exceed ourselves, to strive to transform ourselves into a community of conscience.

We raise our voices to be of use. The work of the poet is for the people.

Notes

1. Pablo Neruda, *Memoirs* (New York: Penguin Books, 1977), p. 53.
2. Pat Mora, "Withdrawal Symptoms," in *Borders* (Houston: Arte Público Press, 1986), p. 26.
3. Elena Poniatowska, "A Question Mark Engraved on My Eyelids," in *The Writer on Her Work: New Essays in New Territory*, ed. Janet Sternberg (New York: W. W. Norton, 1991), p. 85.
4. Neruda, *Memoirs*, p. 49.

ACKNOWLEDGMENTS

I am grateful to the W. K. Kellogg Foundation for the fellowship that allowed me to visit museums, cultural organizations, and indigenous communities in this and other countries. I also wish to thank the University of Iowa, whose support provided the time for completing the essay "University: A Mirage."

I'm not at all sure that without Nicolás Kanellos and Arte Público Press my books of poetry, *Chants*, *Borders*, and *Communion*, would ever have been published. My thanks both to Nick for his steady interest in my work and to his fine assistant, Marina Tristán, for her steady support.

In a few of the more recent essays, I have tried to include references to some of the thinkers and writers who enrich me. Their works merit reading in their entirety.

Teresa McKenna, Elizabeth Mills, and Tey Diana Rebolledo, dear friends, fine teachers, loving, intelligent, strong women, graciously took the time to read drafts of this book. Diana and Libby encouraged me with their warm words, and Teresa covered the manuscript with questions. I send a big grin of gratitude to Dan and Kay Moore, Manuel Pacheco, and my Cincinnati friends Norma Jenckes and Murray Bodo for their always generous faith and affection. My thanks to Vern Scarborough, who lives with my turmoil, and to my sweet family who love me so unconditionally. I love the minds and hearts of each of these people.